The
Celtic
Saints

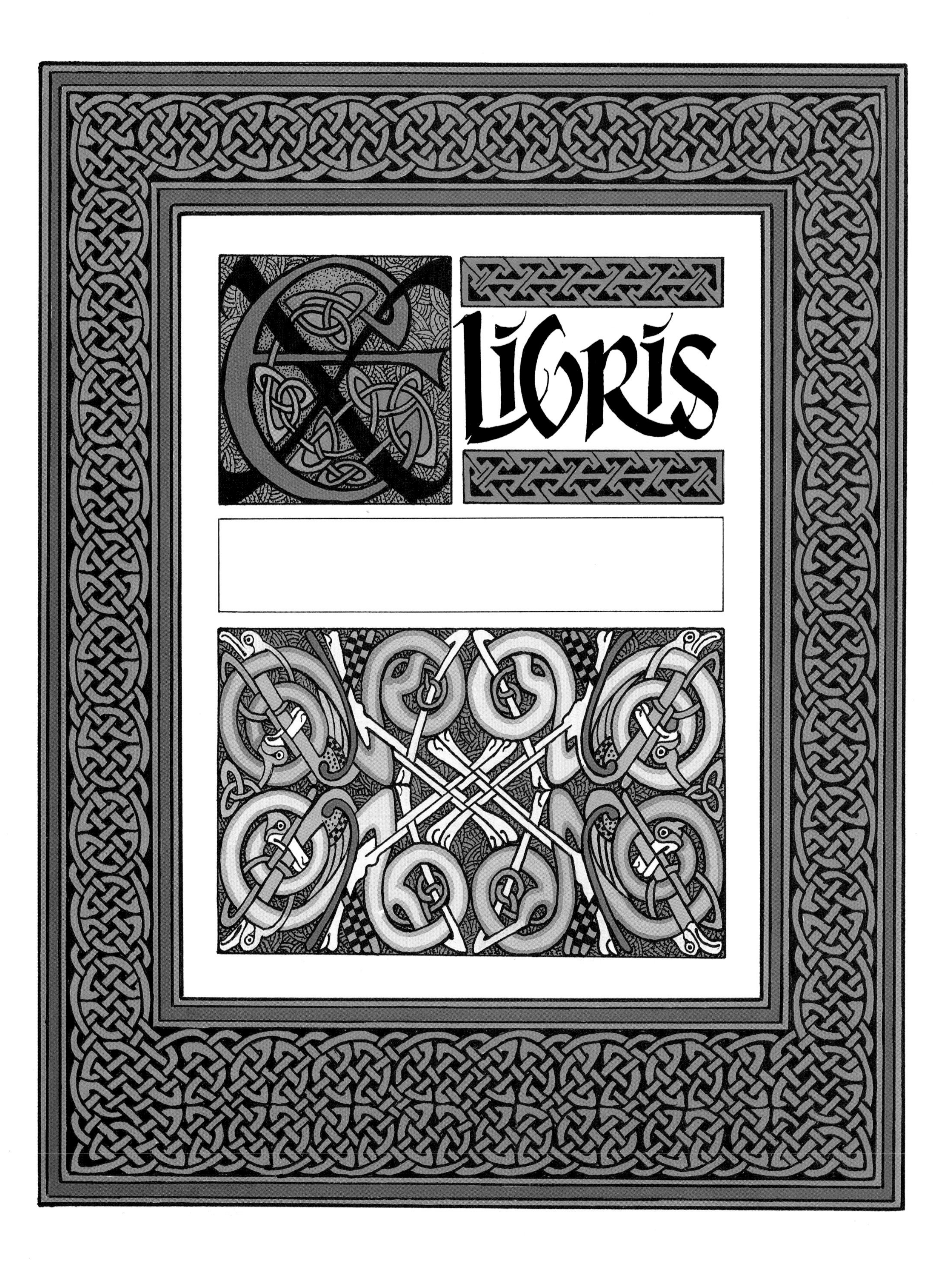
Ex Libris

Dedicated to my son Blaíne

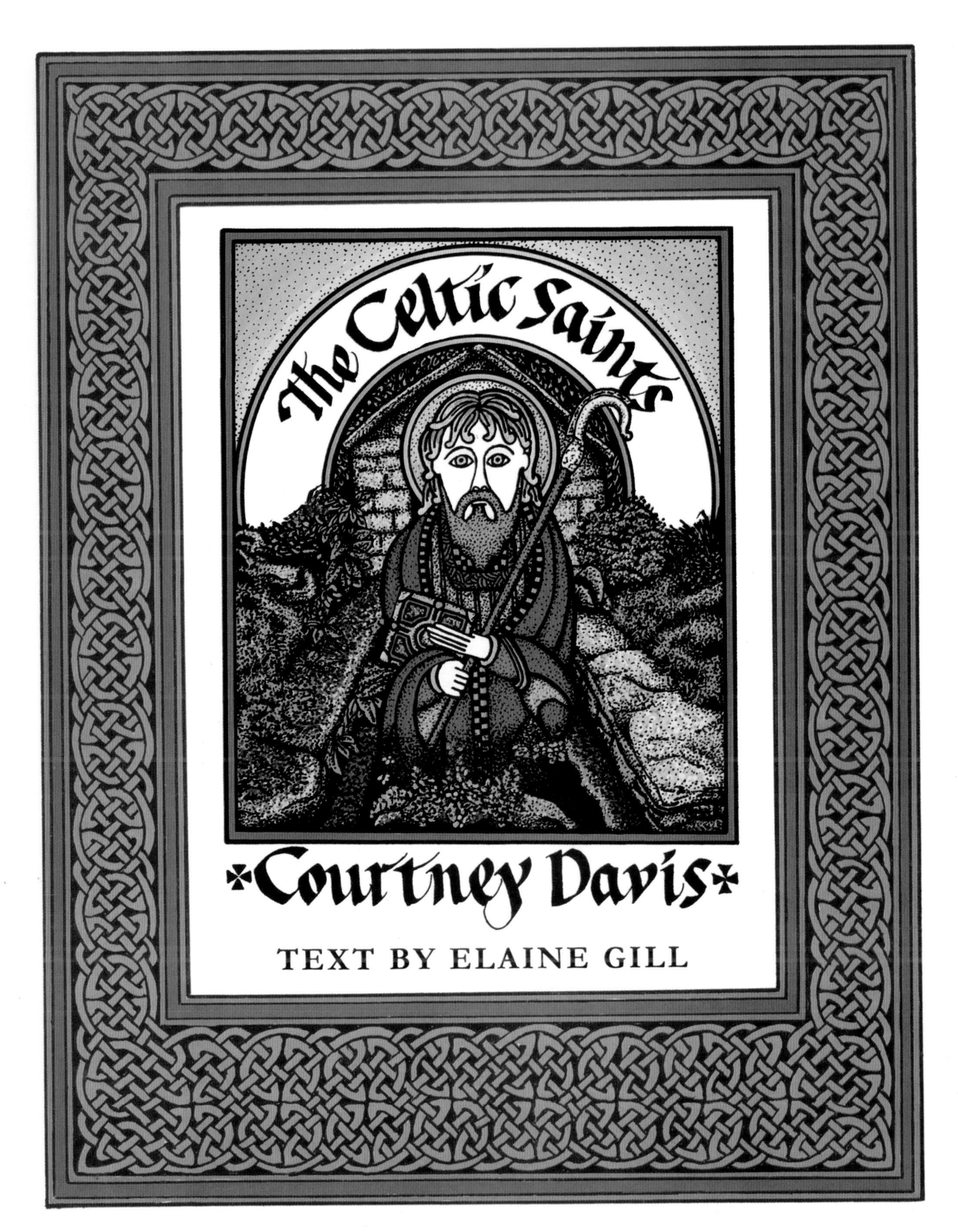

CASSELL&CO

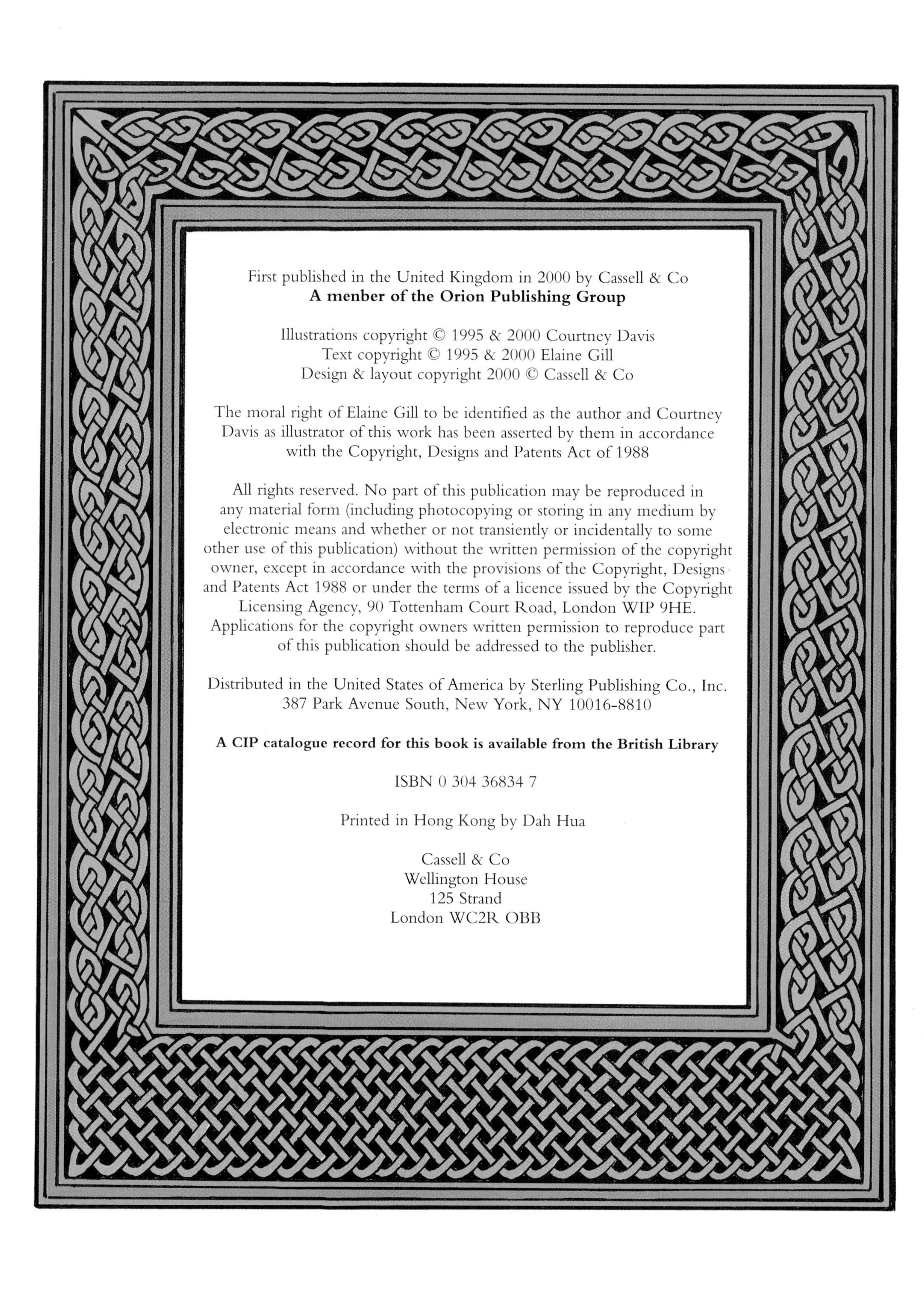

First published in the United Kingdom in 2000 by Cassell & Co
A menber of the Orion Publishing Group

Distributed in the United States of America by Sterling Publishing Co., Inc.
387 Park Avenue South, New York, NY 10016-8810

A CIP catalogue record for this book is available from the British Library

ISBN 0 304 36834 7

Printed in Hong Kong by Dah Hua

Cassell & Co
Wellington House
125 Strand
London WC2R OBB

Contents

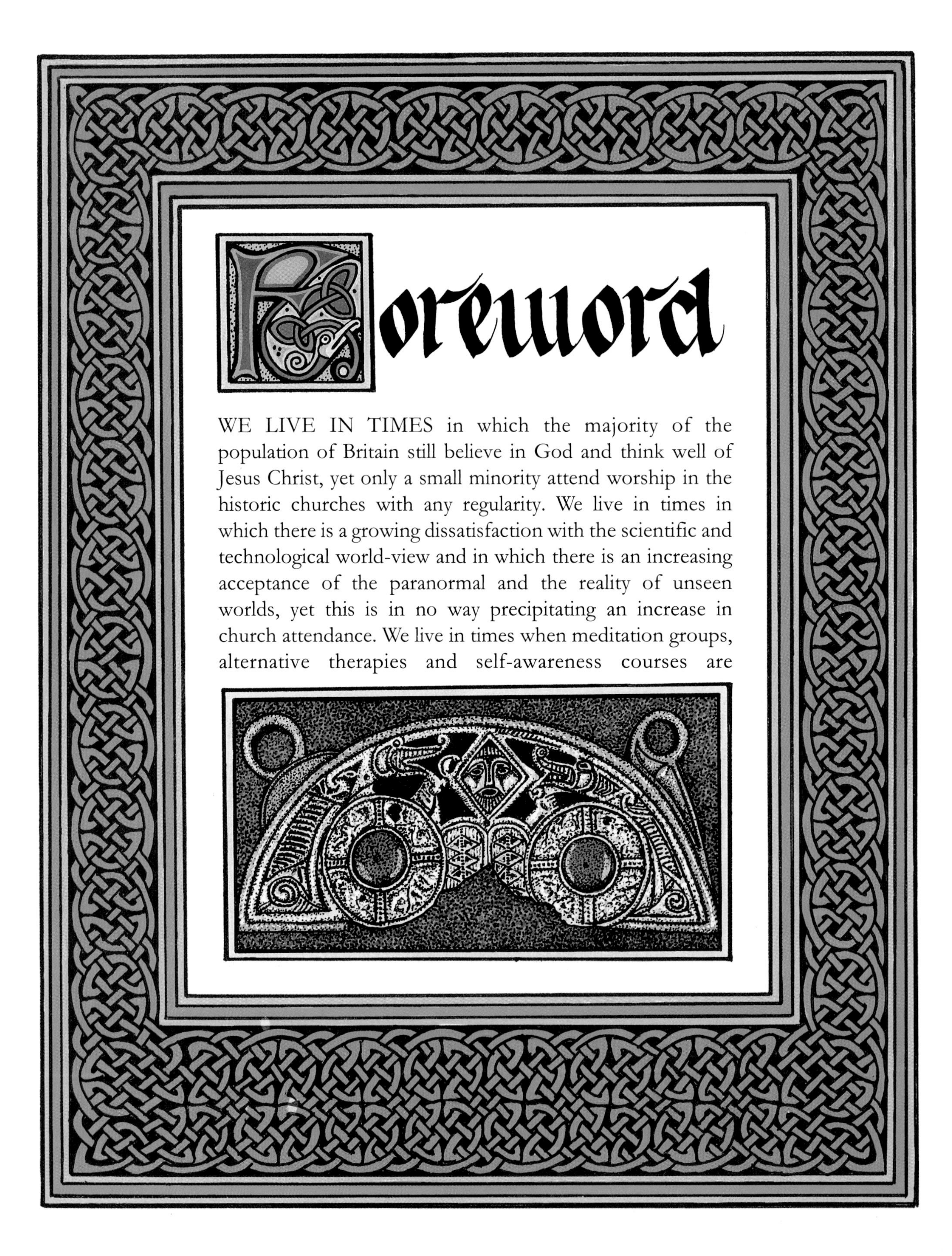

Foreword

WE LIVE IN TIMES in which the majority of the population of Britain still believe in God and think well of Jesus Christ, yet only a small minority attend worship in the historic churches with any regularity. We live in times in which there is a growing dissatisfaction with the scientific and technological world-view and in which there is an increasing acceptance of the paranormal and the reality of unseen worlds, yet this is in no way precipitating an increase in church attendance. We live in times when meditation groups, alternative therapies and self-awareness courses are

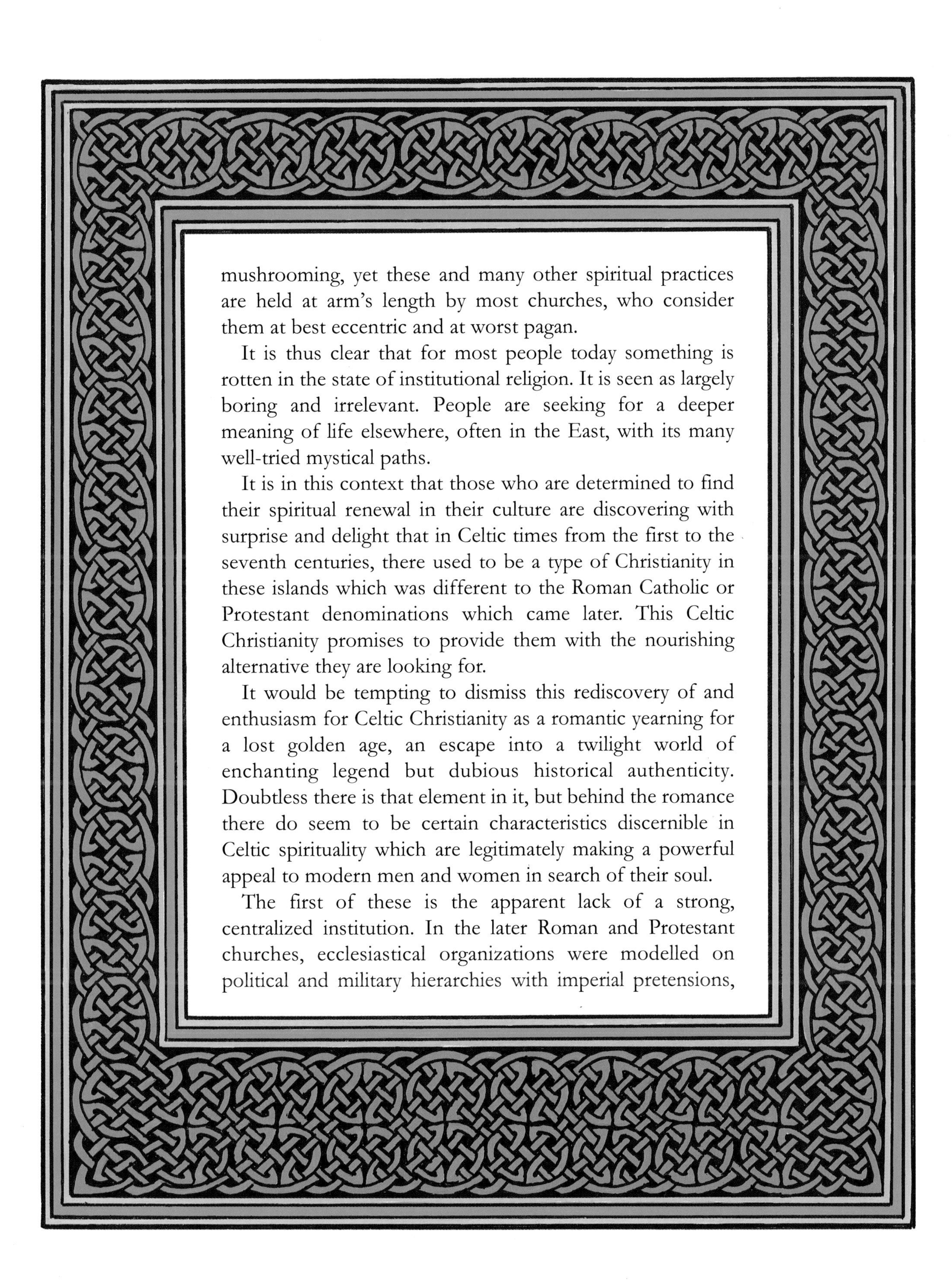

mushrooming, yet these and many other spiritual practices are held at arm's length by most churches, who consider them at best eccentric and at worst pagan.

It is thus clear that for most people today something is rotten in the state of institutional religion. It is seen as largely boring and irrelevant. People are seeking for a deeper meaning of life elsewhere, often in the East, with its many well-tried mystical paths.

It is in this context that those who are determined to find their spiritual renewal in their culture are discovering with surprise and delight that in Celtic times from the first to the seventh centuries, there used to be a type of Christianity in these islands which was different to the Roman Catholic or Protestant denominations which came later. This Celtic Christianity promises to provide them with the nourishing alternative they are looking for.

It would be tempting to dismiss this rediscovery of and enthusiasm for Celtic Christianity as a romantic yearning for a lost golden age, an escape into a twilight world of enchanting legend but dubious historical authenticity. Doubtless there is that element in it, but behind the romance there do seem to be certain characteristics discernible in Celtic spirituality which are legitimately making a powerful appeal to modern men and women in search of their soul.

The first of these is the apparent lack of a strong, centralized institution. In the later Roman and Protestant churches, ecclesiastical organizations were modelled on political and military hierarchies with imperial pretensions,

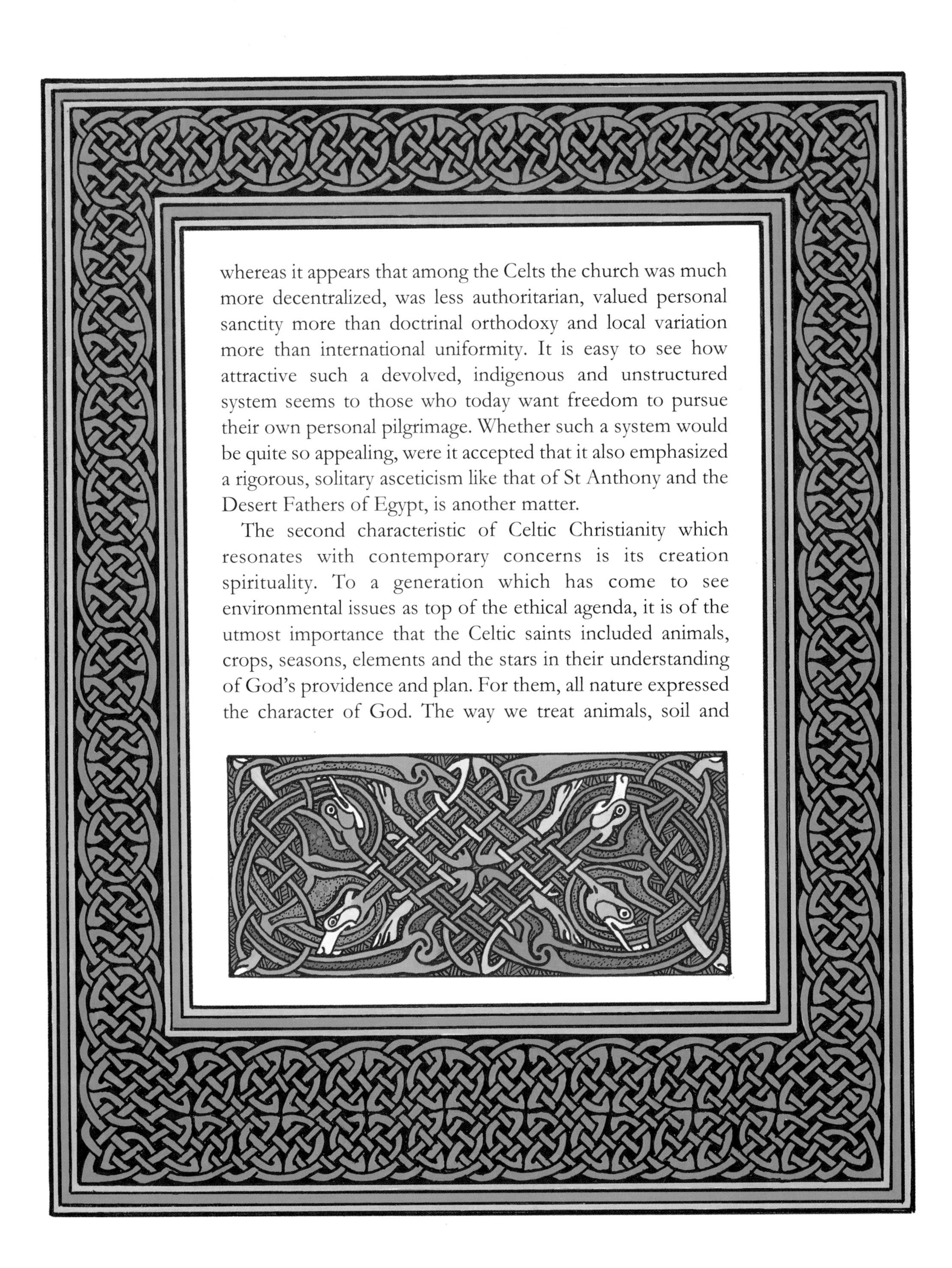

whereas it appears that among the Celts the church was much more decentralized, was less authoritarian, valued personal sanctity more than doctrinal orthodoxy and local variation more than international uniformity. It is easy to see how attractive such a devolved, indigenous and unstructured system seems to those who today want freedom to pursue their own personal pilgrimage. Whether such a system would be quite so appealing, were it accepted that it also emphasized a rigorous, solitary asceticism like that of St Anthony and the Desert Fathers of Egypt, is another matter.

The second characteristic of Celtic Christianity which resonates with contemporary concerns is its creation spirituality. To a generation which has come to see environmental issues as top of the ethical agenda, it is of the utmost importance that the Celtic saints included animals, crops, seasons, elements and the stars in their understanding of God's providence and plan. For them, all nature expressed the character of God. The way we treat animals, soil and

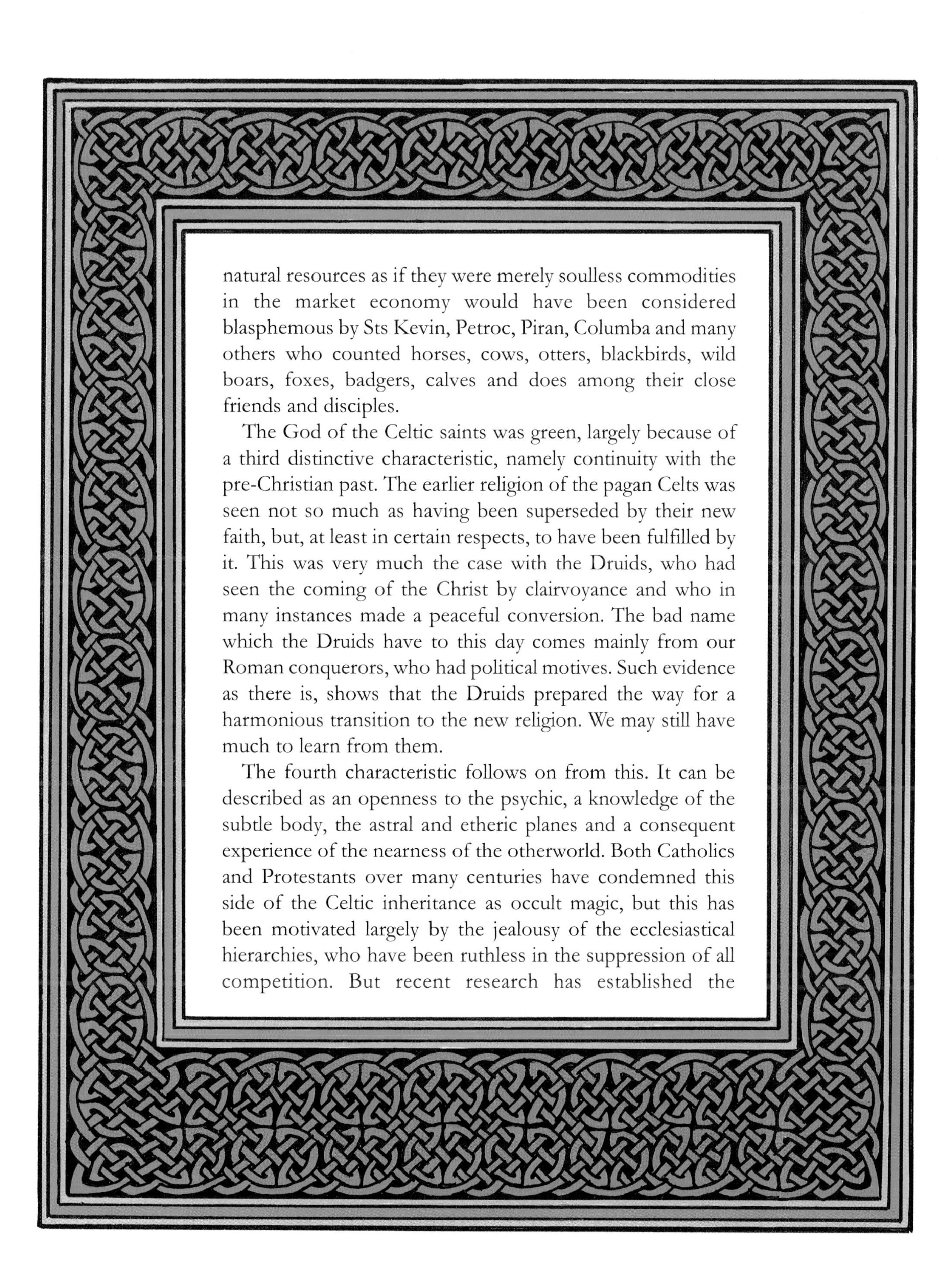

natural resources as if they were merely soulless commodities in the market economy would have been considered blasphemous by Sts Kevin, Petroc, Piran, Columba and many others who counted horses, cows, otters, blackbirds, wild boars, foxes, badgers, calves and does among their close friends and disciples.

The God of the Celtic saints was green, largely because of a third distinctive characteristic, namely continuity with the pre-Christian past. The earlier religion of the pagan Celts was seen not so much as having been superseded by their new faith, but, at least in certain respects, to have been fulfilled by it. This was very much the case with the Druids, who had seen the coming of the Christ by clairvoyance and who in many instances made a peaceful conversion. The bad name which the Druids have to this day comes mainly from our Roman conquerors, who had political motives. Such evidence as there is, shows that the Druids prepared the way for a harmonious transition to the new religion. We may still have much to learn from them.

The fourth characteristic follows on from this. It can be described as an openness to the psychic, a knowledge of the subtle body, the astral and etheric planes and a consequent experience of the nearness of the otherworld. Both Catholics and Protestants over many centuries have condemned this side of the Celtic inheritance as occult magic, but this has been motivated largely by the jealousy of the ecclesiastical hierarchies, who have been ruthless in the suppression of all competition. But recent research has established the

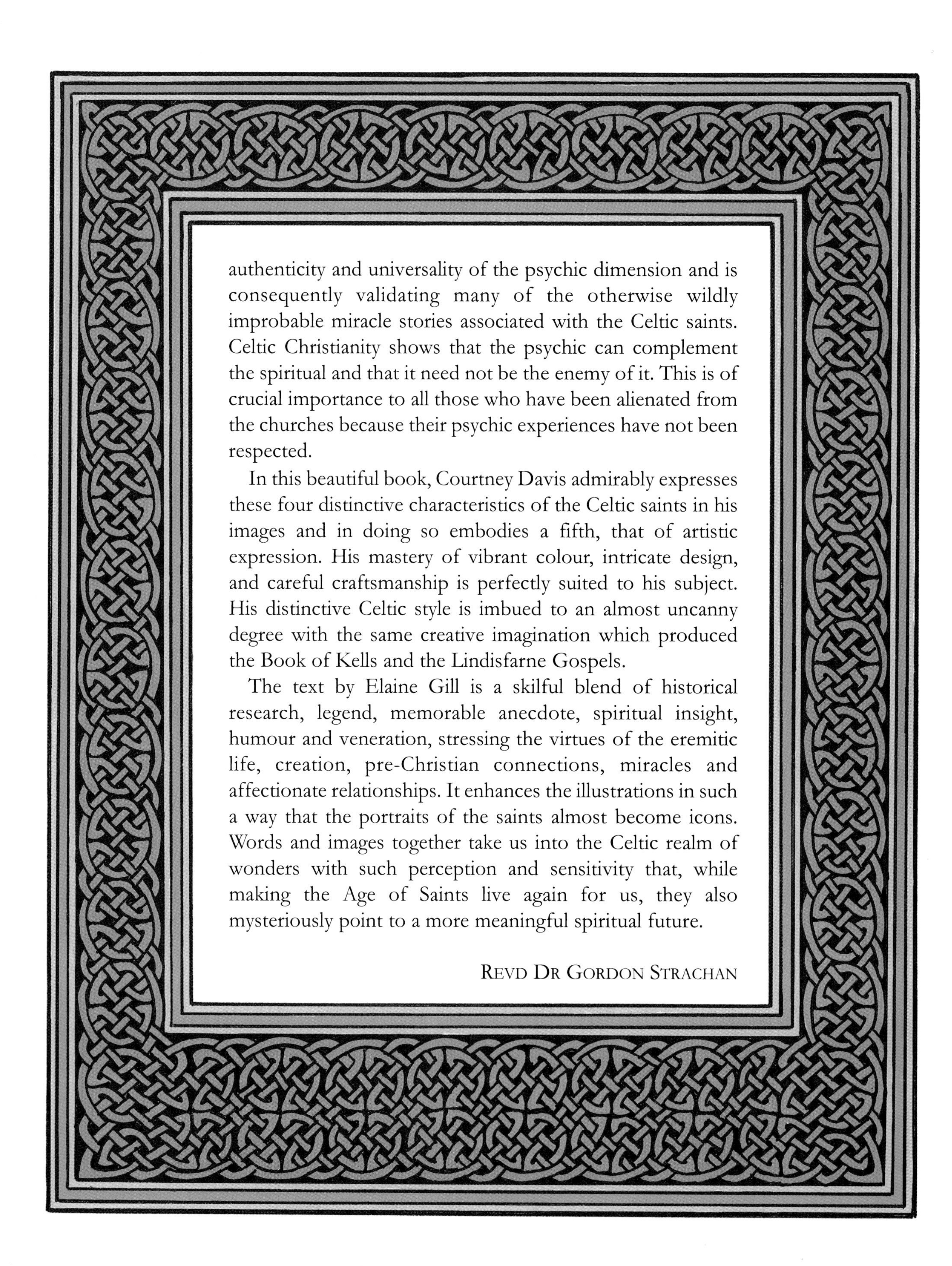

authenticity and universality of the psychic dimension and is consequently validating many of the otherwise wildly improbable miracle stories associated with the Celtic saints. Celtic Christianity shows that the psychic can complement the spiritual and that it need not be the enemy of it. This is of crucial importance to all those who have been alienated from the churches because their psychic experiences have not been respected.

In this beautiful book, Courtney Davis admirably expresses these four distinctive characteristics of the Celtic saints in his images and in doing so embodies a fifth, that of artistic expression. His mastery of vibrant colour, intricate design, and careful craftsmanship is perfectly suited to his subject. His distinctive Celtic style is imbued to an almost uncanny degree with the same creative imagination which produced the Book of Kells and the Lindisfarne Gospels.

The text by Elaine Gill is a skilful blend of historical research, legend, memorable anecdote, spiritual insight, humour and veneration, stressing the virtues of the eremitic life, creation, pre-Christian connections, miracles and affectionate relationships. It enhances the illustrations in such a way that the portraits of the saints almost become icons. Words and images together take us into the Celtic realm of wonders with such perception and sensitivity that, while making the Age of Saints live again for us, they also mysteriously point to a more meaningful spiritual future.

REVD DR GORDON STRACHAN

PREFACE

THE BOOK OF CELTIC SAINTS has proved to be the catalyst of a period of great personal change in my life and coincided with a "trial by fire." Loss of my organization, Spirit of Celtia, which had been a very large part of my life for nearly twenty years, and the constant physical pain following my last operation, had shaken me into re-evaluating where I was going and what I could and could not do in the future.

As I slowed down to match the speed that was most comfortable for my physical body, I soon realized how long it had been since I had been still in my mind *and* body.

With this new mental attitude, I began again to feel closer

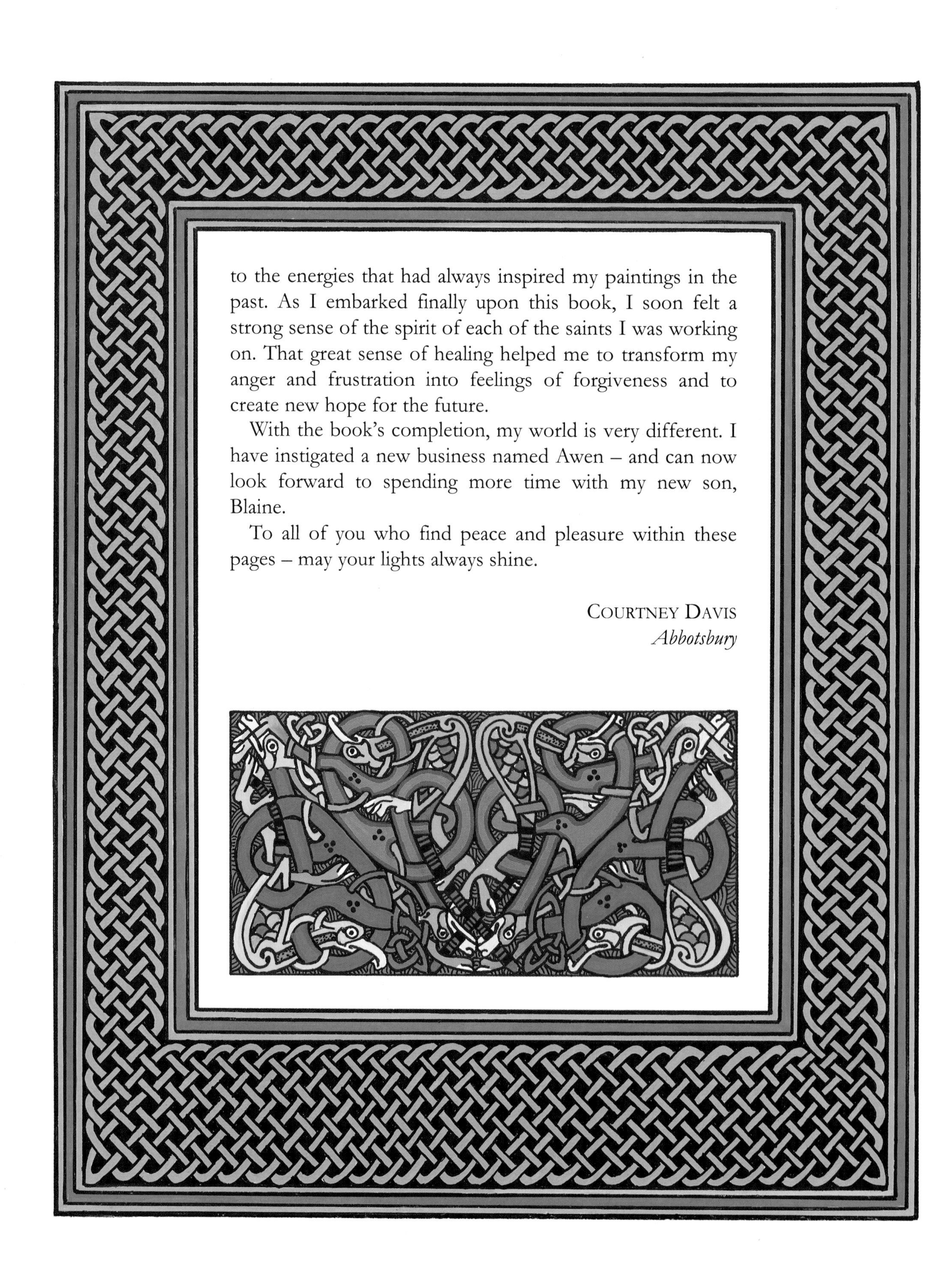

to the energies that had always inspired my paintings in the past. As I embarked finally upon this book, I soon felt a strong sense of the spirit of each of the saints I was working on. That great sense of healing helped me to transform my anger and frustration into feelings of forgiveness and to create new hope for the future.

With the book's completion, my world is very different. I have instigated a new business named Awen – and can now look forward to spending more time with my new son, Blaine.

To all of you who find peace and pleasure within these pages – may your lights always shine.

COURTNEY DAVIS
Abbotsbury

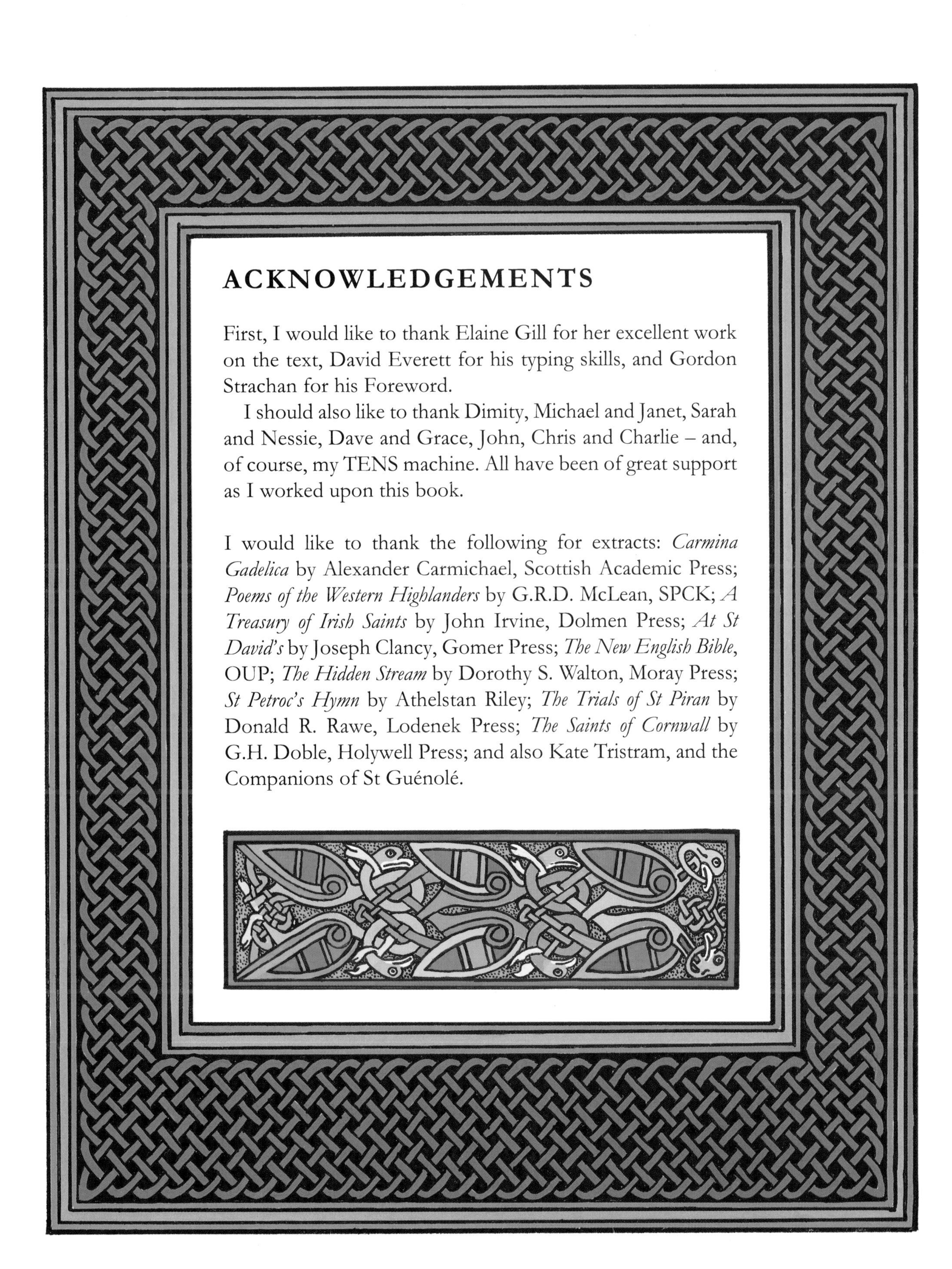

ACKNOWLEDGEMENTS

First, I would like to thank Elaine Gill for her excellent work on the text, David Everett for his typing skills, and Gordon Strachan for his Foreword.

I should also like to thank Dimity, Michael and Janet, Sarah and Nessie, Dave and Grace, John, Chris and Charlie – and, of course, my TENS machine. All have been of great support as I worked upon this book.

I would like to thank the following for extracts: *Carmina Gadelica* by Alexander Carmichael, Scottish Academic Press; *Poems of the Western Highlanders* by G.R.D. McLean, SPCK; *A Treasury of Irish Saints* by John Irvine, Dolmen Press; *At St David's* by Joseph Clancy, Gomer Press; *The New English Bible*, OUP; *The Hidden Stream* by Dorothy S. Walton, Moray Press; *St Petroc's Hymn* by Athelstan Riley; *The Trials of St Piran* by Donald R. Rawe, Lodenek Press; *The Saints of Cornwall* by G.H. Doble, Holywell Press; and also Kate Tristram, and the Companions of St Guénolé.

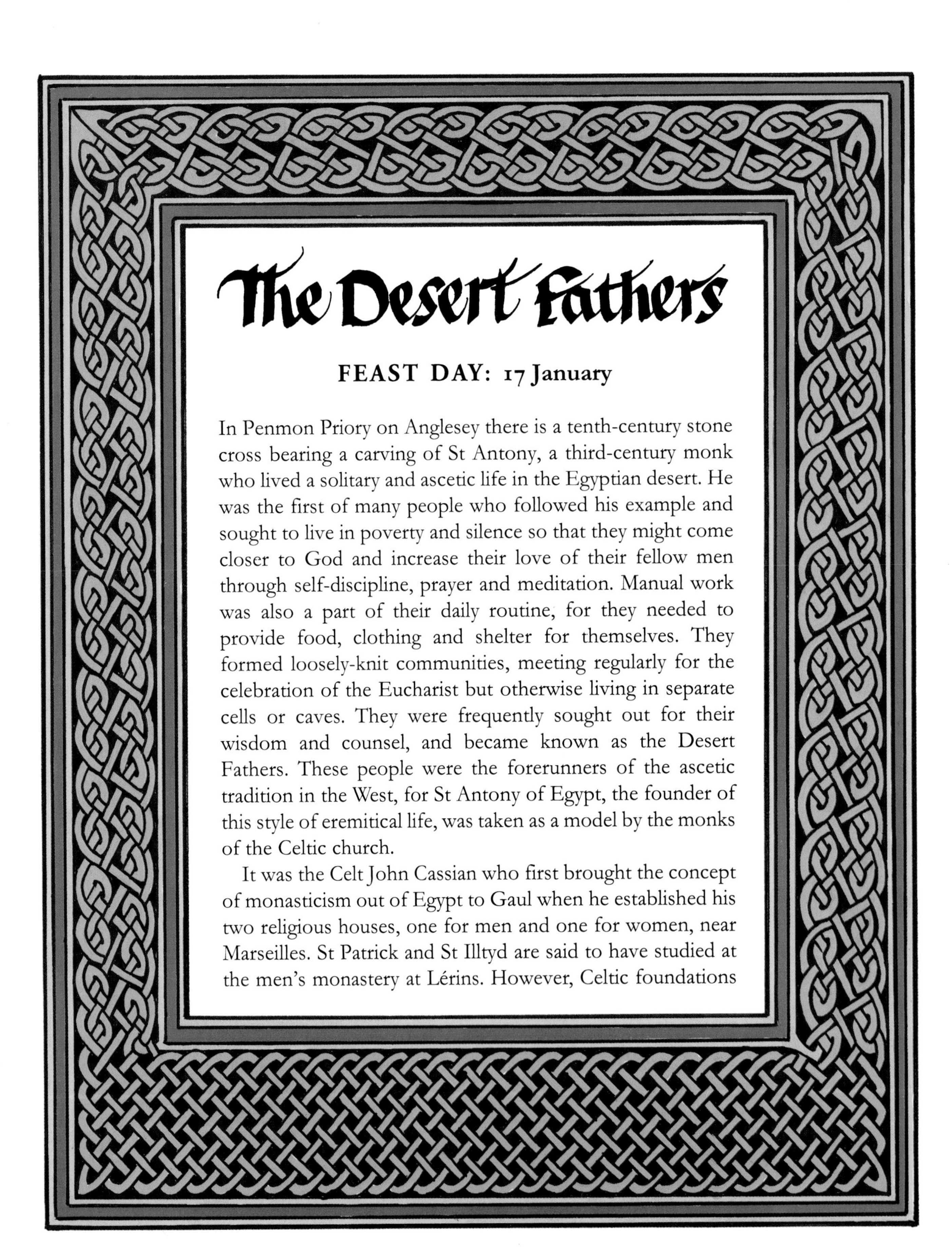

The Desert Fathers

FEAST DAY: 17 January

In Penmon Priory on Anglesey there is a tenth-century stone cross bearing a carving of St Antony, a third-century monk who lived a solitary and ascetic life in the Egyptian desert. He was the first of many people who followed his example and sought to live in poverty and silence so that they might come closer to God and increase their love of their fellow men through self-discipline, prayer and meditation. Manual work was also a part of their daily routine, for they needed to provide food, clothing and shelter for themselves. They formed loosely-knit communities, meeting regularly for the celebration of the Eucharist but otherwise living in separate cells or caves. They were frequently sought out for their wisdom and counsel, and became known as the Desert Fathers. These people were the forerunners of the ascetic tradition in the West, for St Antony of Egypt, the founder of this style of eremitical life, was taken as a model by the monks of the Celtic church.

It was the Celt John Cassian who first brought the concept of monasticism out of Egypt to Gaul when he established his two religious houses, one for men and one for women, near Marseilles. St Patrick and St Illtyd are said to have studied at the men's monastery at Lérins. However, Celtic foundations

in Britain and Ireland evolved directly from the monastery set up by St Martin at Tours, which was subsequently used as a pattern by St Ninian at Whithorn in Galloway. Many Celtic places of retreat and prayer are found on islands or inaccessible coastal promontories, and thus the sea became the equivalent of the sandy wastes of the desert in enhancing isolation and separateness.

This idea was further developed by private places of retreat such as St Ninian's Cave, a few miles from his monastery, and St Cuthbert's place of withdrawal on the Farne Islands.

So it is that a cross on Anglesey depicts an Egyptian monk, in recognition of his enormous influence on Christian practice over many centuries.

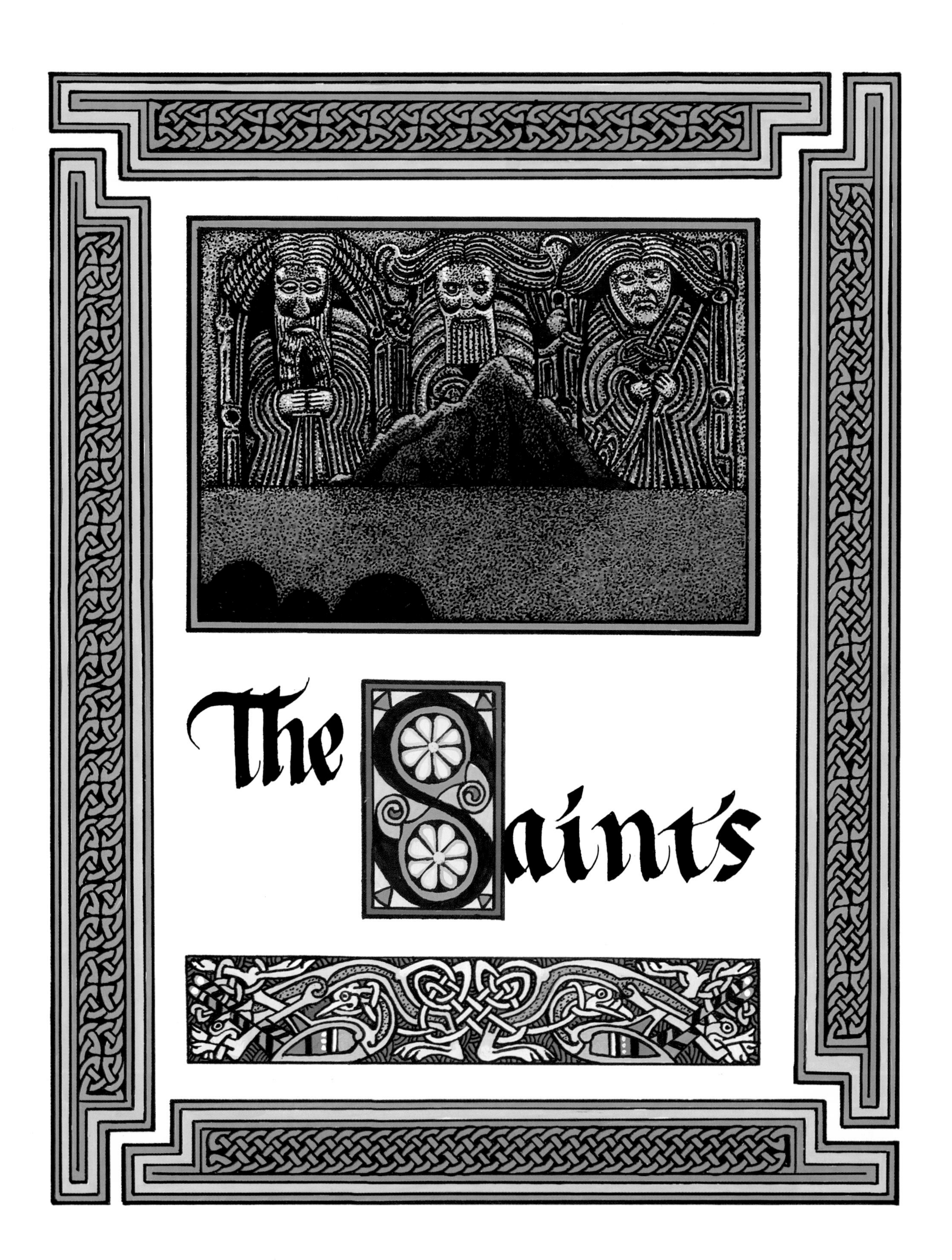
The Saints

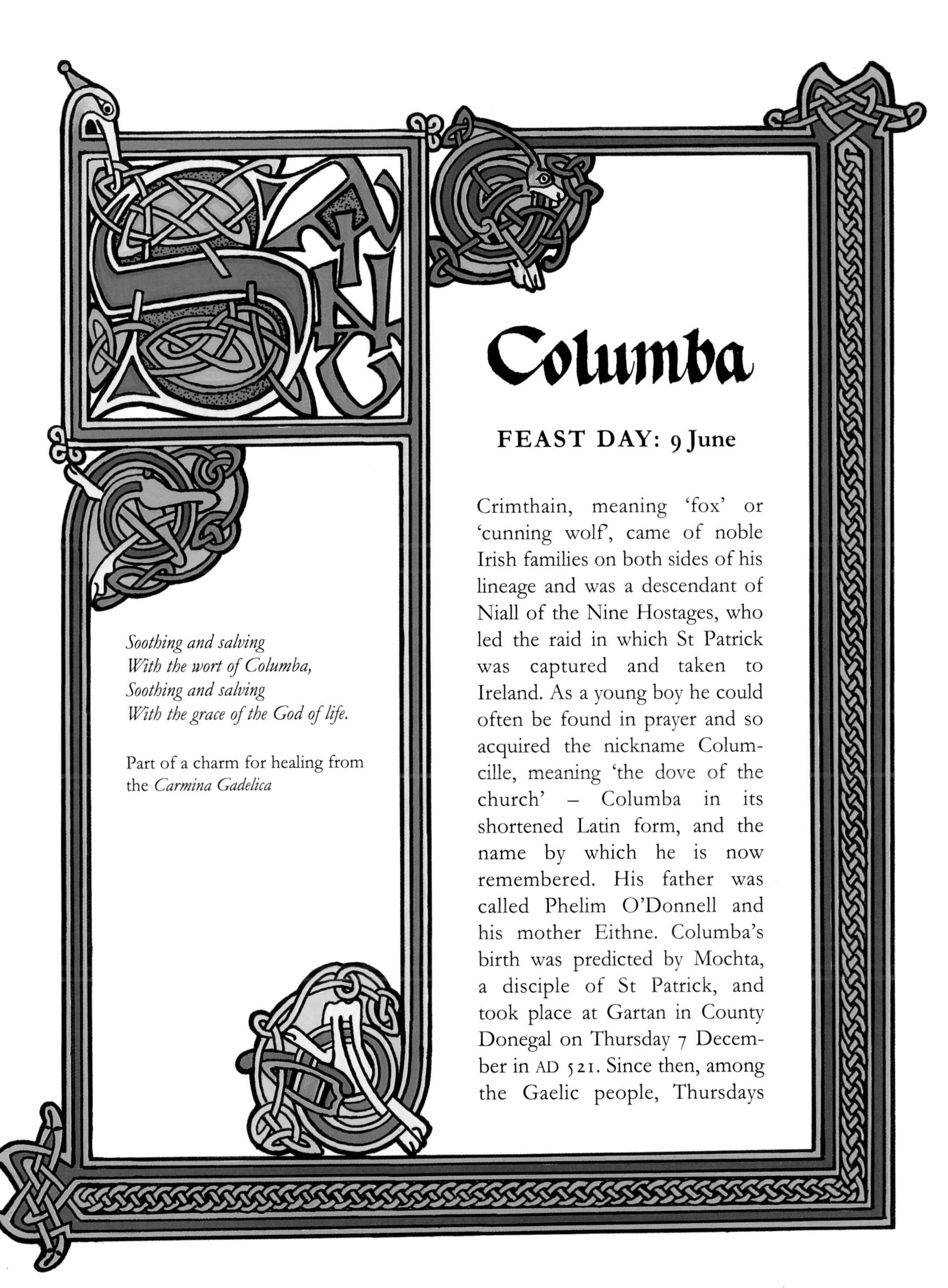

Columba

FEAST DAY: 9 June

Soothing and salving
With the wort of Columba,
Soothing and salving
With the grace of the God of life.

Part of a charm for healing from the *Carmina Gadelica*

Crimthain, meaning 'fox' or 'cunning wolf', came of noble Irish families on both sides of his lineage and was a descendant of Niall of the Nine Hostages, who led the raid in which St Patrick was captured and taken to Ireland. As a young boy he could often be found in prayer and so acquired the nickname Columcille, meaning 'the dove of the church' – Columba in its shortened Latin form, and the name by which he is now remembered. His father was called Phelim O'Donnell and his mother Eithne. Columba's birth was predicted by Mochta, a disciple of St Patrick, and took place at Gartan in County Donegal on Thursday 7 December in AD 521. Since then, among the Gaelic people, Thursdays have been an auspicious day on which to begin a new task or undertaking, such as weaving or starting a journey.

Before Columba's birth his mother, Eithne, had a dream in which she was given a great cloak, displaying many beautiful colours and patterns, which stretched from the coast of Ireland to Scotland. In her vision the magnificent cloak was taken from her by a young man, which made her very sad. However, he returned and told her that she need not grieve, because the dream meant that she would bear a son who would be renowned for his teaching throughout Scotland and Ireland, and so she should be joyful.

In Columba's youth his guardian angel visited him and invited him to choose two virtues. He chose chastity and wisdom, and the third gift of prophecy was bestowed upon him also as a reward for his wise choosing. From childhood he was destined for the priesthood, and he went to the monastery of St Finian at Movilla, at the head of Strangford Lough in County Down, to study theology as well as the arts of copying and illuminating manuscripts. Here he was made a deacon of the church. After a time he travelled on to Leinster and placed himself under the tutelage of the bard Gemman, from whom he learned of poetry and music and many of the ancient traditional tales of Ireland. Some of Columba's own poems are preserved in manuscript form in the Bodleian Library in Oxford.

His studies continued under another Finian at Clonard, and then at the monastery of Mobhi at Glasnevin near Dublin, until in 546, when he was only twenty-five years old, Columba founded his first monastery. It was on the site of a Druid sacred grove at Doire Calgach, later called Doire Cholm Cille for nearly 1,000 years and now known as Derry. Nothing remains of the buildings today, although the round tower stood until as late as 1625. This was the place that Columba loved best and which always remained dearest to his heart. In 533 the monastery of Durrow in County Offaly was established, and then foundations at Kells in County Meath and Moone in County Kildare.

During his ministry, the saint is said to have founded as many as thirty-seven monastic churches in Ireland.

St Columba used his skill as a copyist and illustrator throughout his life. There is a manuscript of the Psalms written in Columba's own hand and known as the 'Cathach' or 'The Battle Book of the O'Donnells' because it was later carried into battle by that family, who claimed the same ancestry. Columba is said to have produced 300 hand-written gospel books altogether, and each time he founded a church, one was given as a gift. He led a party of people on a pilgrimage to the tomb of St Martin at Tours, and he returned with a gospel book that had lain in the earth for a century on St Martin's breast. This became a great treasure of his Derry monastery.

In 561, when Columba was forty years old, he returned to stay with his dear friend Finian at Movilla. Here in the library was a wonderful manuscript known as 'St Martin's Gospel', containing the Mosaic law and the Psalms as well as the four gospels. It was a translation in Latin by St Jerome, copied by Finian while at Whithorn and which St Ninian himself had brought from Gaul. Columba coveted this book greatly and he determined to make a copy of it in secret, night after night. On discovering that Columba had duplicated the book, Finian was outraged and in his anger demanded that the copy should be returned and become the property of Movilla. Columba was displeased at this and demanded that the matter should be taken to the court of the High King Diarmid for him to pronounce judgement. After hearing both sides the King ruled with these words: 'To every cow its calf, to every book its copy' – meaning that the original and Columba's copy both belonged to Finian.

Columba refused to accept this decision and rallied his friends and members of his clan and family to support him against King Diarmid. The opposing sides met in a valley near Sligo where the mighty battle of Cuildrevne was fought, resulting in the slaughter of many thousands of men. Diarmid was defeated, but Columba was filled with remorse when he realized at what cost he had won his victory.

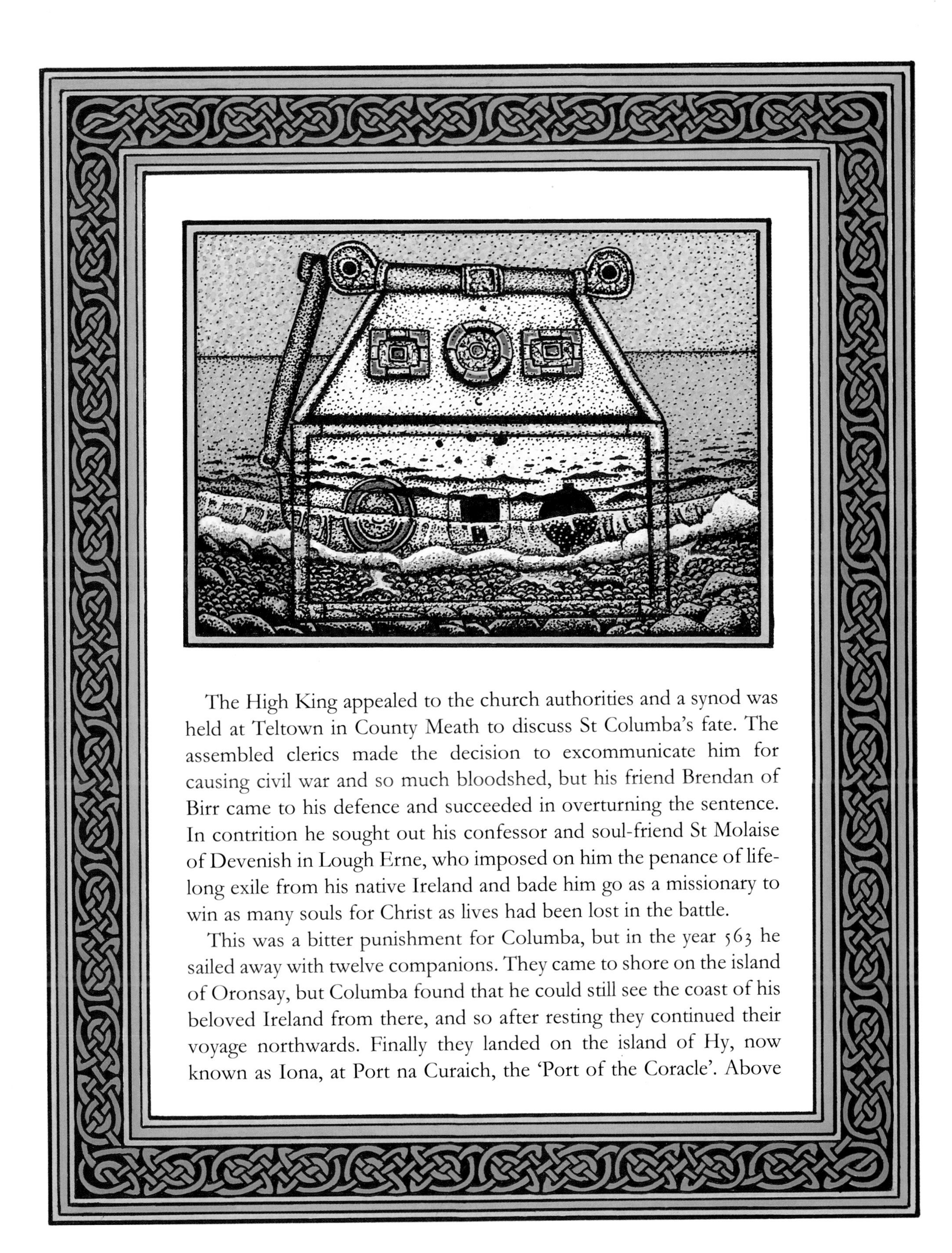

The High King appealed to the church authorities and a synod was held at Teltown in County Meath to discuss St Columba's fate. The assembled clerics made the decision to excommunicate him for causing civil war and so much bloodshed, but his friend Brendan of Birr came to his defence and succeeded in overturning the sentence. In contrition he sought out his confessor and soul-friend St Molaise of Devenish in Lough Erne, who imposed on him the penance of life-long exile from his native Ireland and bade him go as a missionary to win as many souls for Christ as lives had been lost in the battle.

This was a bitter punishment for Columba, but in the year 563 he sailed away with twelve companions. They came to shore on the island of Oronsay, but Columba found that he could still see the coast of his beloved Ireland from there, and so after resting they continued their voyage northwards. Finally they landed on the island of Hy, now known as Iona, at Port na Curaich, the 'Port of the Coracle'. Above this bay there is a pile of stones known to this day as the 'Cairn of the Back Turned to Ireland', which the saint climbed to assure himself that he could no longer see his native land. Odhrain of Latteragh, who had died thirteen years before and was Columba's cousin, had already founded a church here, and in the cemetery known as Rilig Odhrain the Irish kings of Dalriada were buried.

The monastery on Iona became St Columba's chief foundation and for many years, until superseded by St Andrew, he was the patron saint of Scotland. Many missionary journeys were undertaken from Iona, and on one occasion Columba travelled north to visit Brude, a Pictish king. The King refused the little band admission to his fortress and the great doors were barred against them. However, the saint made the sign of the cross and the gates swung open, allowing them to enter. Brude and Columba became firm friends and the chieftain was instrumental in securing the tenure of Iona for the monks.

Columba loved all of creation and was very close to the natural world. Combined with his gift of seership, this enabled him to help his fellow creatures, both man and animal, in an extraordinary way. One day he called one of the brothers to him and told him that in three days' time he was to wait on the western side of Iona for a crane which would be blown off course and arrive hungry and exhausted on the shore. The monk was further instructed to carry the creature tenderly to a nearby house and to nurse and feed it for three days and nights. It happened just as Columba had predicted and, the rescue having been accomplished, the grateful bird, fully recovered, took to the air and flew away to Ireland.

Another time, as the saint was reading in his cell, a robin came and perched on a nearby ledge, singing sweetly. Columba listened to its piping song and not only heard the notes but seemed to understand a story of how a similar bird had been present at the Crucifixion. The little creature had perched on the crown of thorns and tried to pull them out of Jesus' bleeding brow, and this is how the bird which was formerly all brown came to have a red breast.

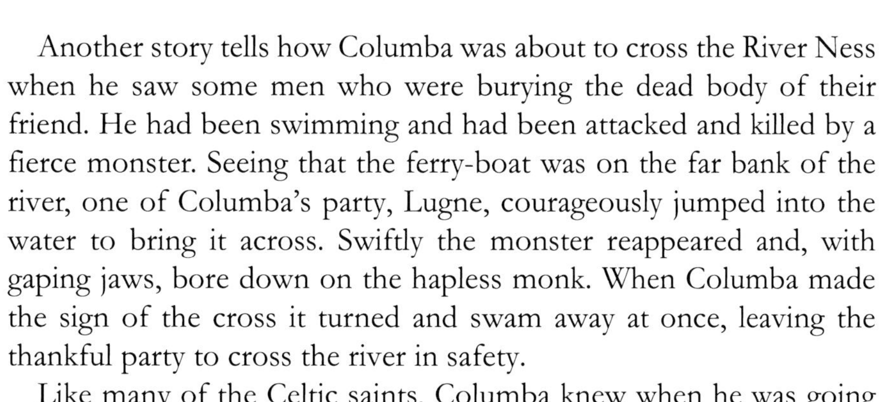

Another story tells how Columba was about to cross the River Ness when he saw some men who were burying the dead body of their friend. He had been swimming and had been attacked and killed by a fierce monster. Seeing that the ferry-boat was on the far bank of the river, one of Columba's party, Lugne, courageously jumped into the water to bring it across. Swiftly the monster reappeared and, with gaping jaws, bore down on the hapless monk. When Columba made the sign of the cross it turned and swam away at once, leaving the thankful party to cross the river in safety.

Like many of the Celtic saints, Columba knew when he was going to die. He told his brethren that he had longed to leave this world at Eastertide but that he had not wanted to turn the feast into a time of mourning for them and so had waited a little longer. On his last day on earth he was taken in a cart out to the fields where his monks were toiling, and here he blessed the grain and crops. An old white horse which had faithfully served the brothers for many years approached him and, gently resting his head on Columba's shoulder, was seen to weep tears at the saint's impending departure from this world.

Later in the day Columba attempted some manuscript copying, but on reaching the tenth verse of Psalm 34, 'but those who seek the Lord lack no good thing', he laid aside his pen, declaring that someone else would have to finish the task. It was 9 June in the year 597, the very year that St Augustine was sent from Rome and landed in Kent. He was buried on Iona, but it is said that his body was later taken to Downpatrick to lie in a grave along with those of St Patrick and St Brigid. Each year on his feast day, 9 June, a three-mile pilgrimage or 'turas' takes place at Glencolmcille.

The first and most well-known biography of Columba was written only about a century after his death by Adamnan, one of his successors as Abbot of Iona, and it contains many instances of the miraculous powers of the saint. One story is of an apple tree which grew on the south side of the monastery at Derry. It was prolific but bore only very bitter fruit. After Columba blessed the tree the apples

became sweet and edible.

An interesting historical link with the present day is that when in 574 Columba consecrated and anointed his friend Aidan as the Christian king of the Irish people in Scotland, he set a precedent which has been followed down the ages and is still continuing in the coronation ceremonies held in Westminster Abbey today.

As we have seen, Columba possessed the gift of prophecy and a famous stanza attributed to him runs,

Iona of my heart,
Iona of my love,
Instead of monks' voices
Shall be lowing of cattle;
But ere the world come to an end,
Iona shall be as it was.

Today the abbey has been rebuilt and there is once more a Christian community on the island of Iona.

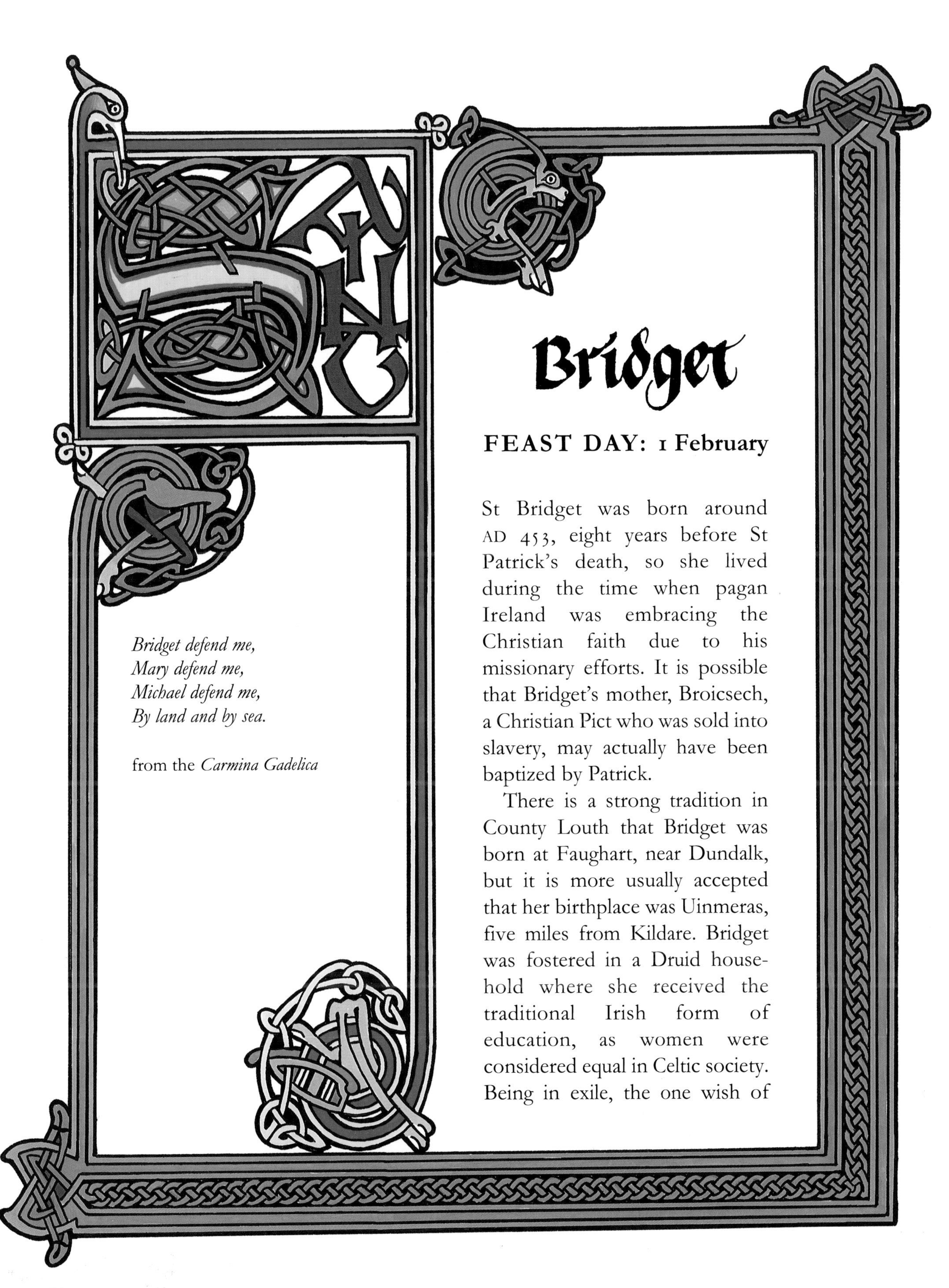

Bridget

FEAST DAY: 1 February

Bridget defend me,
Mary defend me,
Michael defend me,
By land and by sea.

from the *Carmina Gadelica*

St Bridget was born around AD 453, eight years before St Patrick's death, so she lived during the time when pagan Ireland was embracing the Christian faith due to his missionary efforts. It is possible that Bridget's mother, Broicsech, a Christian Pict who was sold into slavery, may actually have been baptized by Patrick.

There is a strong tradition in County Louth that Bridget was born at Faughart, near Dundalk, but it is more usually accepted that her birthplace was Uinmeras, five miles from Kildare. Bridget was fostered in a Druid household where she received the traditional Irish form of education, as women were considered equal in Celtic society. Being in exile, the one wish of mother and daughter was to return to Dubthach, Bridget's father, who was a pagan chieftain of Leinster.

When Bridget was twelve years of age her mother's sight began to fail, and it became the young girl's task to take care of a large herd of cattle and to do all the milking and the making of butter and cream. The owner of the cattle, their master, was so pleased with the way that Bridget tended them and went about her other work that he offered to give her the cows. Instead of accepting, she asked if she and her mother might be given their freedom so that they could go home. Their wish was duly granted and they rejoined Dubthach, thanking God as they did so. Later their former master, to whom Bridget had explained the Christian message, was himself baptized. Statues of the saint often portray her with a milk-cow lying at her feet.

In the course of time her father chose for her someone whom he considered to be a suitable husband. The young man was a poet, and in Celtic social structure bards were second only to kings. However, Bridget had a deep desire to become a nun and to dedicate her life to God, so she chose to go to an abbey instead.

At the clothing ceremony, conducted by Bishop Macaille and Bishop Mel when she was fourteen years old, Bridget and seven others who also wished to become nuns were given habits of white wool to put on. This rite marked the institution of the first formal community of Christian women in Ireland, and the white homespun cloth became the distinctive dress of Irish nuns for many centuries. They were each asked to choose one of the Beatitudes (the sayings of Jesus from the Sermon on the Mount) which would have special meaning for them. Bridget chose 'Blessed are the merciful, for they shall obtain mercy' as her particular text, and throughout her life her open-handed generosity and her compassion more than met the needs of those who came to her for help.

She did not live in solitude like so many of the Celtic saints but was a familiar sight on the Curragh of Kildare, where the Irish kings raced their horses even then. She also travelled widely and frequently

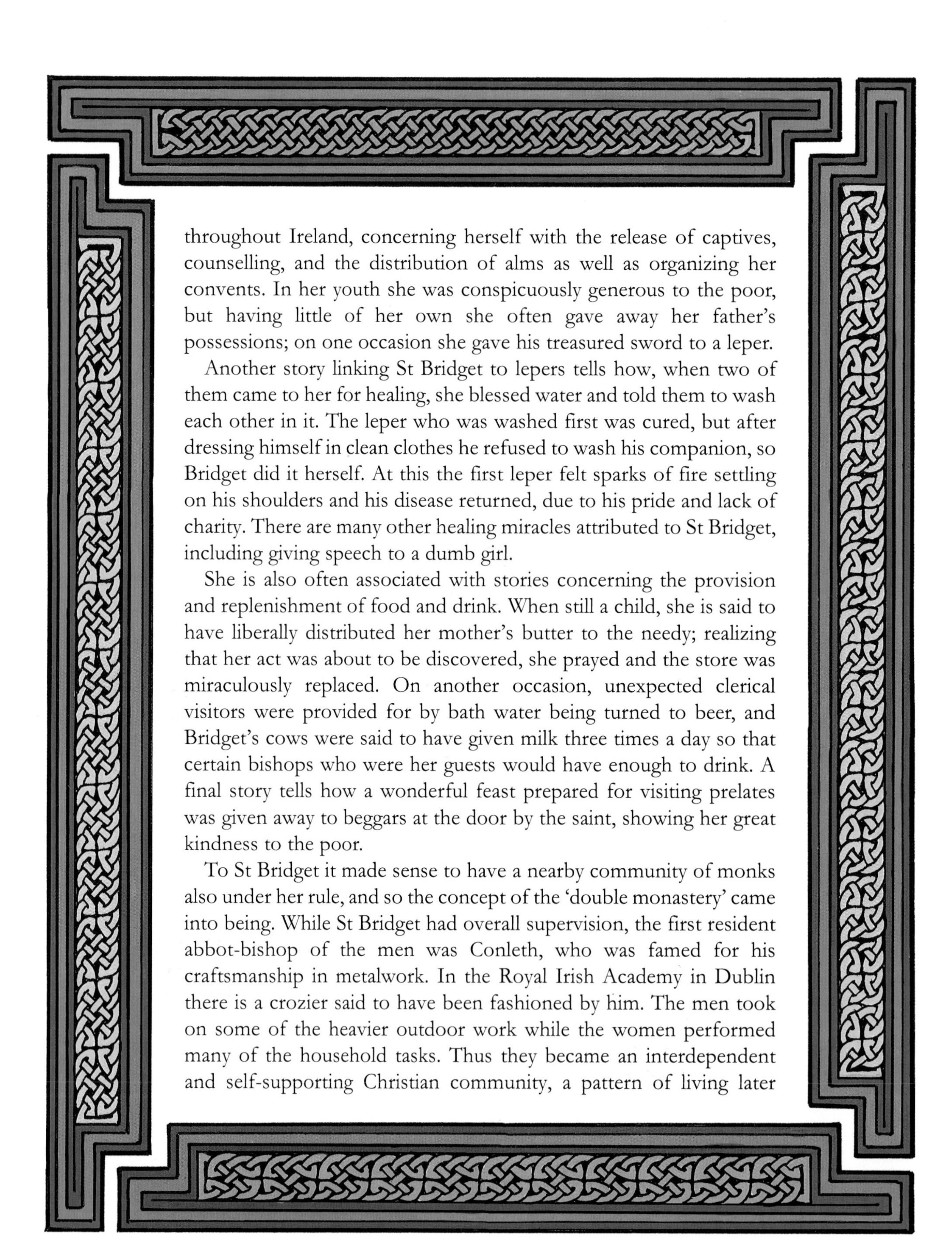

throughout Ireland, concerning herself with the release of captives, counselling, and the distribution of alms as well as organizing her convents. In her youth she was conspicuously generous to the poor, but having little of her own she often gave away her father's possessions; on one occasion she gave his treasured sword to a leper.

Another story linking St Bridget to lepers tells how, when two of them came to her for healing, she blessed water and told them to wash each other in it. The leper who was washed first was cured, but after dressing himself in clean clothes he refused to wash his companion, so Bridget did it herself. At this the first leper felt sparks of fire settling on his shoulders and his disease returned, due to his pride and lack of charity. There are many other healing miracles attributed to St Bridget, including giving speech to a dumb girl.

She is also often associated with stories concerning the provision and replenishment of food and drink. When still a child, she is said to have liberally distributed her mother's butter to the needy; realizing that her act was about to be discovered, she prayed and the store was miraculously replaced. On another occasion, unexpected clerical visitors were provided for by bath water being turned to beer, and Bridget's cows were said to have given milk three times a day so that certain bishops who were her guests would have enough to drink. A final story tells how a wonderful feast prepared for visiting prelates was given away to beggars at the door by the saint, showing her great kindness to the poor.

To St Bridget it made sense to have a nearby community of monks also under her rule, and so the concept of the 'double monastery' came into being. While St Bridget had overall supervision, the first resident abbot-bishop of the men was Conleth, who was famed for his craftsmanship in metalwork. In the Royal Irish Academy in Dublin there is a crozier said to have been fashioned by him. The men took on some of the heavier outdoor work while the women performed many of the household tasks. Thus they became an interdependent and self-supporting Christian community, a pattern of living later

taken as a model by St Hilda of Whitby. Generous as ever, when Conleth died Bridget gave away his cherished vestments, brought from Rome, to a poor church in need.

St Bridget's first convent was built on the Liffey plain at Kildare, on land given to her by her friend the King of Leinster. It was on the site of an ancient pagan sanctuary marked by a large oak tree. Indeed, the name Kildare means 'Church of the Oak Tree', and in time it became the principal church of the kingdom. Nothing remains now of Bridget's monastic settlement here, but a round tower with a Romanesque porch marks its site.

Bridget died in about 524, and was buried in a casket of precious metal studded with jewels to the right of the high altar. It is thought that in 835, during the Danish invasions, her mortal remains were removed to Downpatrick to lie with those of St Columba and St Patrick, but there is no proof of this.

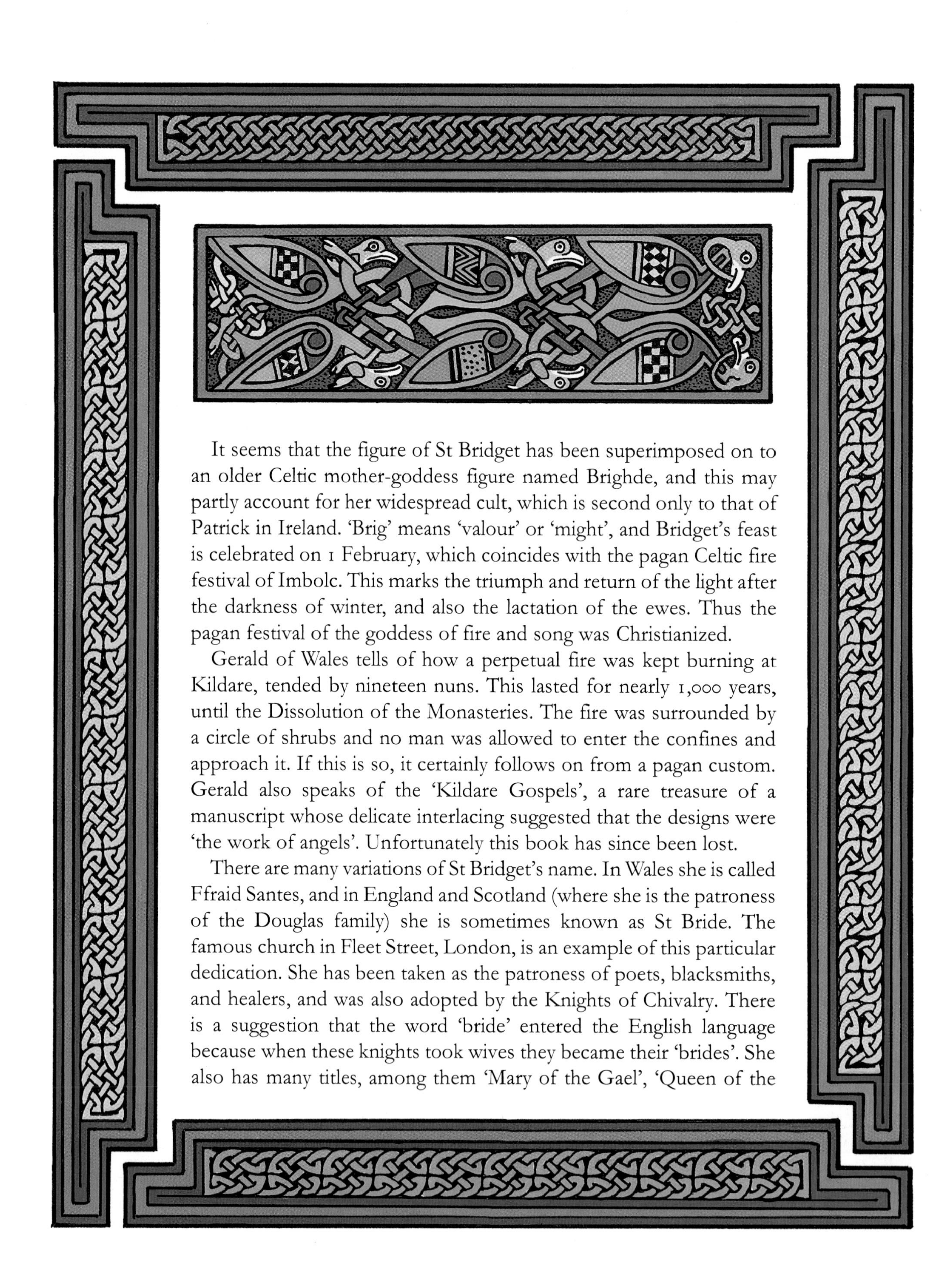

It seems that the figure of St Bridget has been superimposed on to an older Celtic mother-goddess figure named Brighde, and this may partly account for her widespread cult, which is second only to that of Patrick in Ireland. 'Brig' means 'valour' or 'might', and Bridget's feast is celebrated on 1 February, which coincides with the pagan Celtic fire festival of Imbolc. This marks the triumph and return of the light after the darkness of winter, and also the lactation of the ewes. Thus the pagan festival of the goddess of fire and song was Christianized.

Gerald of Wales tells of how a perpetual fire was kept burning at Kildare, tended by nineteen nuns. This lasted for nearly 1,000 years, until the Dissolution of the Monasteries. The fire was surrounded by a circle of shrubs and no man was allowed to enter the confines and approach it. If this is so, it certainly follows on from a pagan custom. Gerald also speaks of the 'Kildare Gospels', a rare treasure of a manuscript whose delicate interlacing suggested that the designs were 'the work of angels'. Unfortunately this book has since been lost.

There are many variations of St Bridget's name. In Wales she is called Ffraid Santes, and in England and Scotland (where she is the patroness of the Douglas family) she is sometimes known as St Bride. The famous church in Fleet Street, London, is an example of this particular dedication. She has been taken as the patroness of poets, blacksmiths, and healers, and was also adopted by the Knights of Chivalry. There is a suggestion that the word 'bride' entered the English language because when these knights took wives they became their 'brides'. She also has many titles, among them 'Mary of the Gael', 'Queen of the

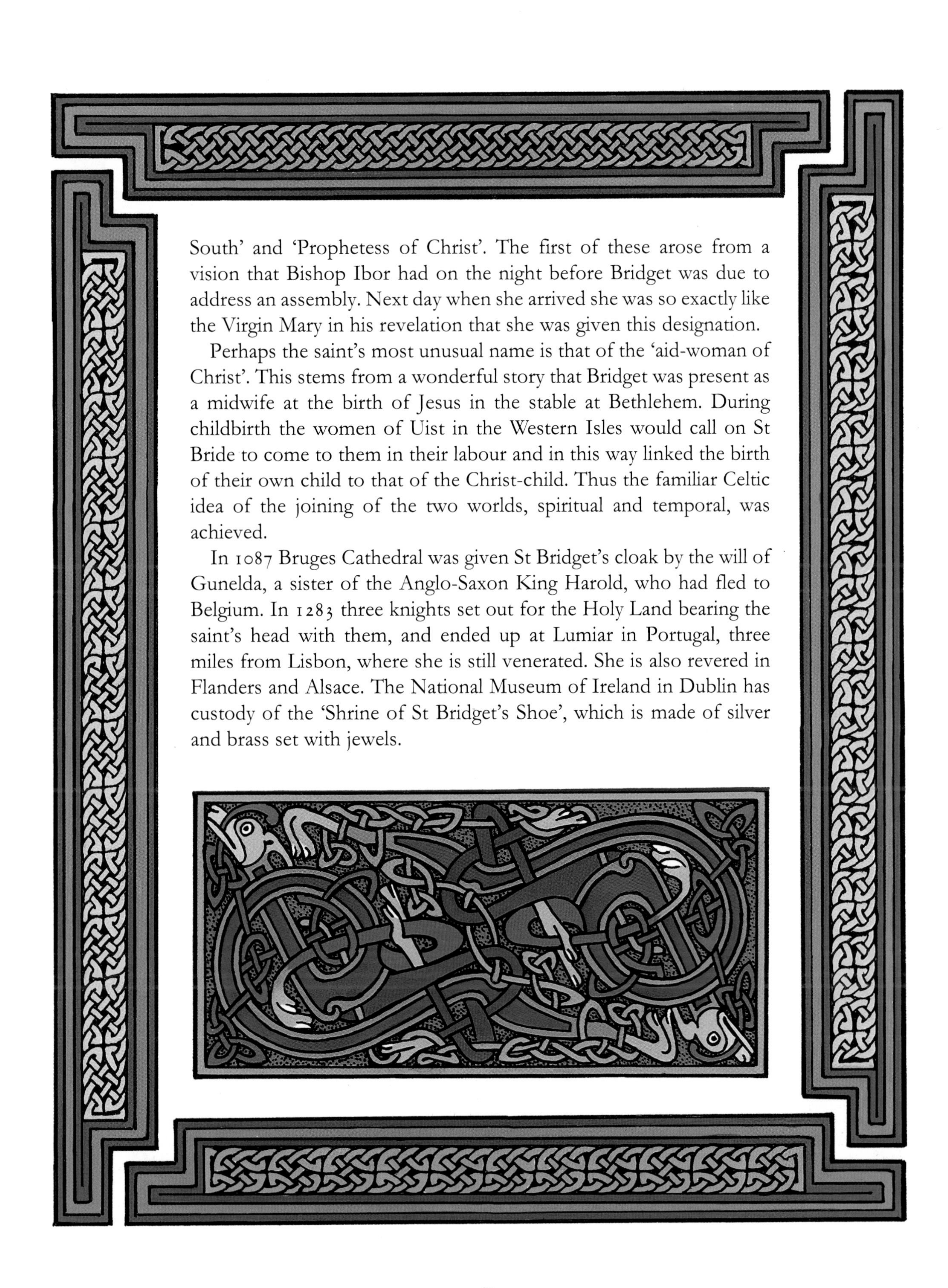

South' and 'Prophetess of Christ'. The first of these arose from a vision that Bishop Ibor had on the night before Bridget was due to address an assembly. Next day when she arrived she was so exactly like the Virgin Mary in his revelation that she was given this designation.

Perhaps the saint's most unusual name is that of the 'aid-woman of Christ'. This stems from a wonderful story that Bridget was present as a midwife at the birth of Jesus in the stable at Bethlehem. During childbirth the women of Uist in the Western Isles would call on St Bride to come to them in their labour and in this way linked the birth of their own child to that of the Christ-child. Thus the familiar Celtic idea of the joining of the two worlds, spiritual and temporal, was achieved.

In 1087 Bruges Cathedral was given St Bridget's cloak by the will of Gunelda, a sister of the Anglo-Saxon King Harold, who had fled to Belgium. In 1283 three knights set out for the Holy Land bearing the saint's head with them, and ended up at Lumiar in Portugal, three miles from Lisbon, where she is still venerated. She is also revered in Flanders and Alsace. The National Museum of Ireland in Dublin has custody of the 'Shrine of St Bridget's Shoe', which is made of silver and brass set with jewels.

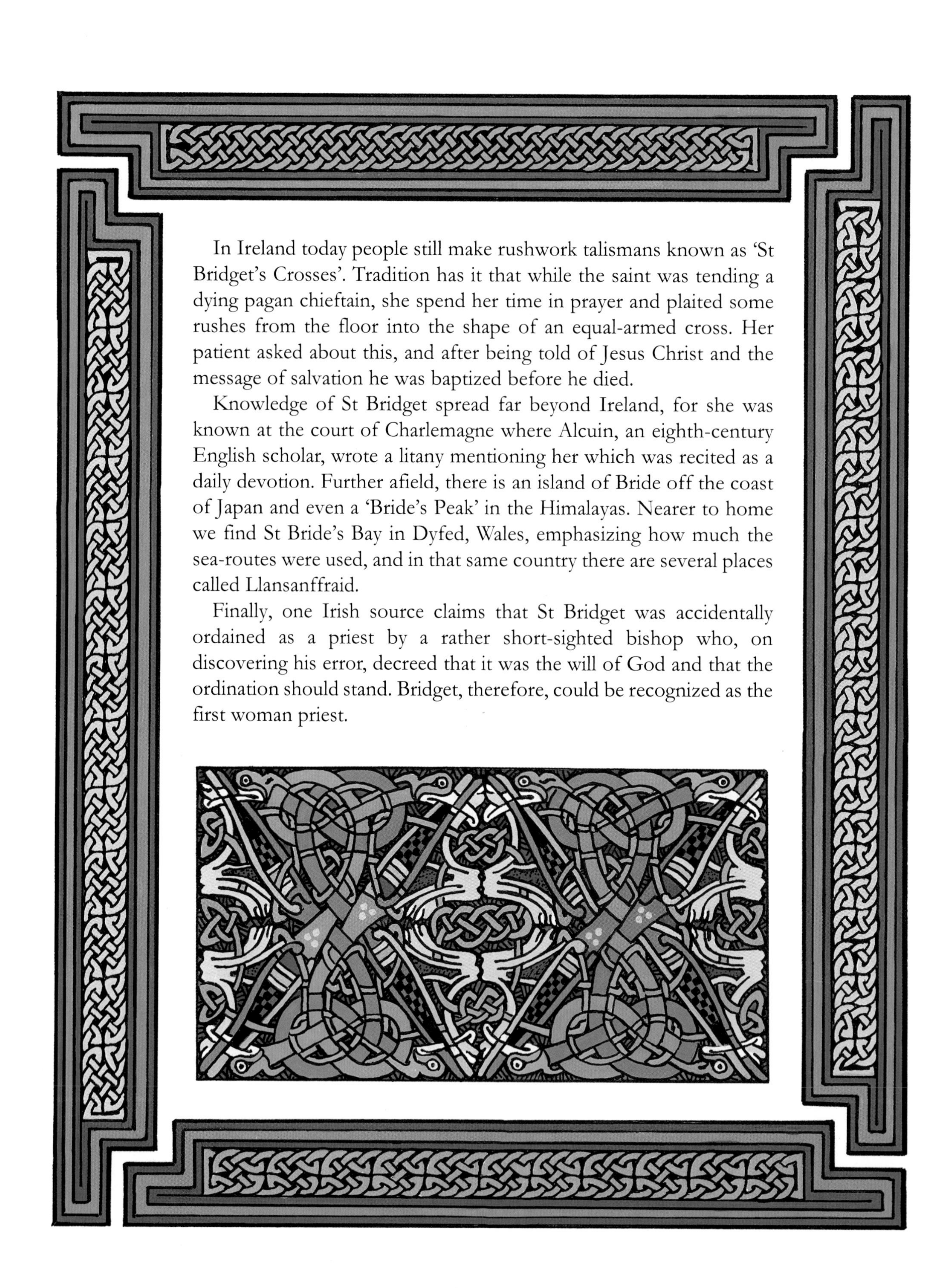

In Ireland today people still make rushwork talismans known as 'St Bridget's Crosses'. Tradition has it that while the saint was tending a dying pagan chieftain, she spend her time in prayer and plaited some rushes from the floor into the shape of an equal-armed cross. Her patient asked about this, and after being told of Jesus Christ and the message of salvation he was baptized before he died.

Knowledge of St Bridget spread far beyond Ireland, for she was known at the court of Charlemagne where Alcuin, an eighth-century English scholar, wrote a litany mentioning her which was recited as a daily devotion. Further afield, there is an island of Bride off the coast of Japan and even a 'Bride's Peak' in the Himalayas. Nearer to home we find St Bride's Bay in Dyfed, Wales, emphasizing how much the sea-routes were used, and in that same country there are several places called Llansanffraid.

Finally, one Irish source claims that St Bridget was accidentally ordained as a priest by a rather short-sighted bishop who, on discovering his error, decreed that it was the will of God and that the ordination should stand. Bridget, therefore, could be recognized as the first woman priest.

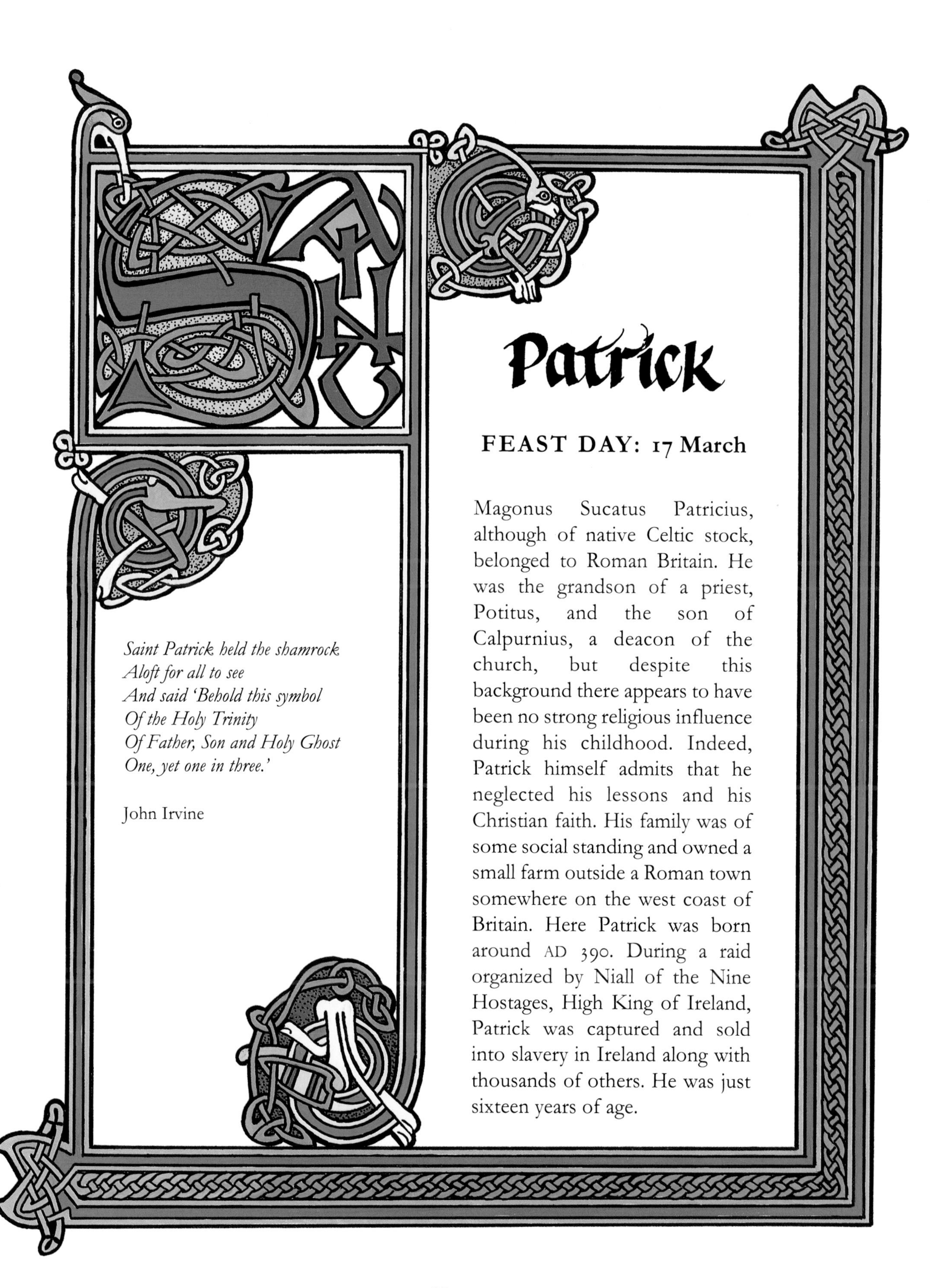

Patrick

FEAST DAY: 17 March

Saint Patrick held the shamrock
Aloft for all to see
And said 'Behold this symbol
Of the Holy Trinity
Of Father, Son and Holy Ghost
One, yet one in three.'

John Irvine

Magonus Sucatus Patricius, although of native Celtic stock, belonged to Roman Britain. He was the grandson of a priest, Potitus, and the son of Calpurnius, a deacon of the church, but despite this background there appears to have been no strong religious influence during his childhood. Indeed, Patrick himself admits that he neglected his lessons and his Christian faith. His family was of some social standing and owned a small farm outside a Roman town somewhere on the west coast of Britain. Here Patrick was born around AD 390. During a raid organized by Niall of the Nine Hostages, High King of Ireland, Patrick was captured and sold into slavery in Ireland along with thousands of others. He was just sixteen years of age.

For six years he tended the beasts of his wealthy Pictish master, Miliuc, on the slopes of Sliabh Mis, Slemish Mountain in County Antrim. Here in the silence and the loneliness, often in snow, frost and rain, he learned to turn to God for help and strength, and fervent prayer became a vital part of his life. It is possible that he was baptized by Caranoc, a successor of St Ninian at Whithorn, during this period. Spurred on by dreams and an inner voice telling him to go home, he escaped and walked 200 miles to a seaport at the mouth of the River Vartry near Wicklow, where he joined a ship carrying Irish hunting hounds to Gaul.

After three days they landed, probably in Gaul, and travelled for a further twenty-eight days through deserted country. Both men and dogs were weak from lack of food and the sea-captain challenged Patrick to ask his God to provide nourishment for them all. Almost at once a herd of pigs appeared on the road in answer to his prayer, and for the remainder of the journey they were all well supplied with food as well as being blessed with fine weather.

After this adventure Patrick eventually made his way home to his family in Britain. However, he could not settle and became convinced that he was being called back to Ireland. To prepare himself properly, he travelled to the Continent for education and training, retracing his steps to Gaul. There is a tradition that he studied at Lérins on the island of St Honorat, and evidence of him being a pupil at Auxerre. Here he was ordained deacon by Amator, a predecessor of St Germanus, and was taught by them both. Germanus was sent to Britain by Pope Celestine I and became increasingly aware of the great need for teaching and organization in Ireland.

Patrick had received messages in dreams, through an angelic figure and soul-friend called Victor, from the voice of the Irish, asking him to 'come and walk once more among us'. It was therefore suggested that Patrick should be sent, and his hopes were high, but the proposal was rejected because of his relative illiteracy, and one Palladius was consecrated bishop and sent instead. Some time later the authorities

reconsidered and decided that Patrick might be useful as an assistant to Palladius. Accordingly he set off, accompanied by a senior priest called Segitius. They had gone only sixteen miles towards the coast when news of Palladius' death reached them. Here, at Avrolles, Patrick was consecrated bishop and embarked on the work for which he had waited so long.

Tradition has it that he landed in Ireland in AD 432 at the narrow entrance to Strangford Lough, not far from the area he had known as a captive. 'Saul' in Irish means 'barn', and it was at this place that Dichu, a local lord, gave him land and just such a building for his first church and also became his first convert.

Later Padraig, as he is known in Irish, lived in the region of the former capital of Ulster at Emain Macha and at Ard Macha, the present-day Armagh, which still claims descent from him. King Daire held court here and Patrick set up his church within the royal rath. It grew into a monastery which is now the site of the cathedral.

Easter Day, 25 March 433, saw him confronting the pagan Druids by lighting a paschal or Easter fire. This act coincided with the Druidic spring festival, when all the fires in the land were extinguished and then relit from the one fire burning on the Hill of Tara, the royal residence and pagan sacred place. The outraged Druids saw Patrick's fire burning on the distant slopes of Slane and prophetically warned King Laoghaire that if it was not put out very quickly then the light of Christ would never be extinguished in Erin.

As a consequence of his challenge to Druidical authority, a trial of powers was arranged between the saint and the Druid magician Lucetmael. Initially the magician tried to overcome Patrick with poison, waist-deep snow and thick darkness, but to no avail. For the next round a trial by water was suggested by the High King, who wanted the matter resolved. He proposed that a book from each of the parties should be submerged and that he would worship the God of whichever one was unharmed. Patrick was willing but Lucetmael was not. Similarly he would not agree to the books being cast into a fire.

Patrick then put forward a scheme which seemed to favour the Druid. A hut was to be constructed in two sections, one half of dry wood and the other half of green wood. Lucetmael was invited to stand inside the green part wearing the saint's cloak while Benen, a follower of Patrick, would enter the dry half wearing the mantle of the Druid. The shelter would then be set on fire. According to legend, Lucetmael was completely consumed in the flames but not Patrick's cloak, while on the other side only the Druid's cloak was burned to ashes. Despite this, Laoghaire himself died a pagan, but his brother, Conal Gulban, became Patrick's disciple and protector.

The best-known story of Patrick is surely his association with the shamrock plant, the three-leaved symbol of the Irish nation, by which he is said to have explained the idea of the Holy Trinity to the High King's daughters in Connacht.

During his life Patrick baptized many thousands of people and nurtured a love of the religious life which he had enjoyed during his training on the Continent. He was responsible for the organization and ordering of the church under episcopal rule and was constantly travelling the country teaching, preaching, and faithfully spreading the gospel.

In the church at St Patrice, a village near Tours in France, there is a statue of Patrick and also a stained-glass window above the altar which illustrates the tale that the saint came here in midwinter. Tired and cold from travelling, he settled down beneath a frost-covered tree to rest. As he slept the tree burst into bloom, shedding light and warmth. It continued to flower each year in December until it was destroyed a century or so ago. This story is reminiscent of the 'Holy Thorn' at Glastonbury, which also flowers annually during the dark days of winter.

Depictions of Patrick generally show him with snakes at his feet, recalling the legend that he banished all the serpents, presumably representing evil, from the land; indeed, snakes of any kind are unknown in Ireland.

On the last Sunday in July each year, in County Mayo, the pilgrimage to Cruachan Aigli, or Croagh Patrick as it is now known, takes place. The old name means 'hill of the eagles', and it is a steep mountain 2,500 feet high. Patrick is said to have spent the whole of one Lent season here in prayer and fasting, appealing to God for the conversion of the Irish. Thousands of pilgrims, some barefoot, make the long trek up the stony path to the top in memory of his devotion and vigil.

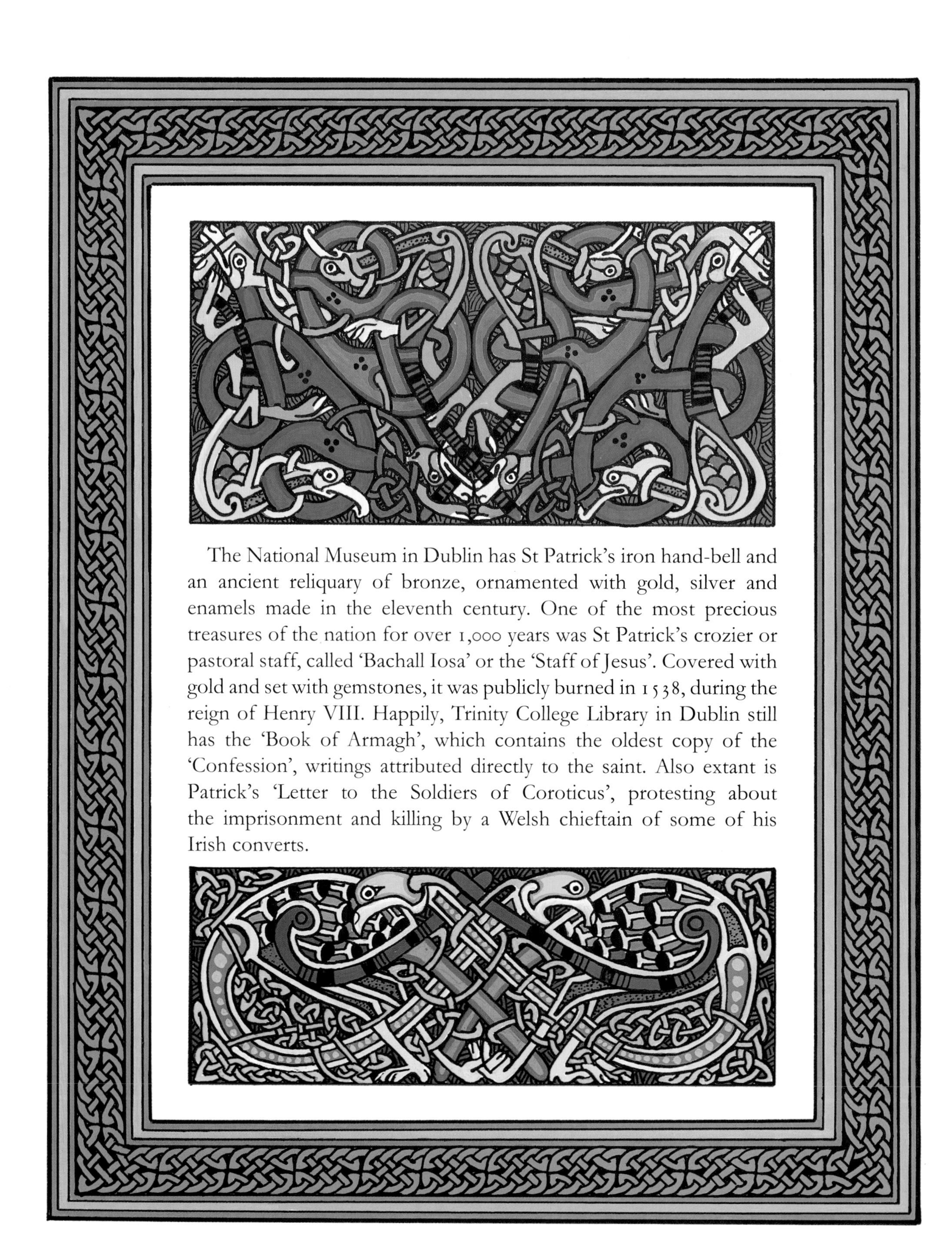

The National Museum in Dublin has St Patrick's iron hand-bell and an ancient reliquary of bronze, ornamented with gold, silver and enamels made in the eleventh century. One of the most precious treasures of the nation for over 1,000 years was St Patrick's crozier or pastoral staff, called 'Bachall Iosa' or the 'Staff of Jesus'. Covered with gold and set with gemstones, it was publicly burned in 1538, during the reign of Henry VIII. Happily, Trinity College Library in Dublin still has the 'Book of Armagh', which contains the oldest copy of the 'Confession', writings attributed directly to the saint. Also extant is Patrick's 'Letter to the Soldiers of Coroticus', protesting about the imprisonment and killing by a Welsh chieftain of some of his Irish converts.

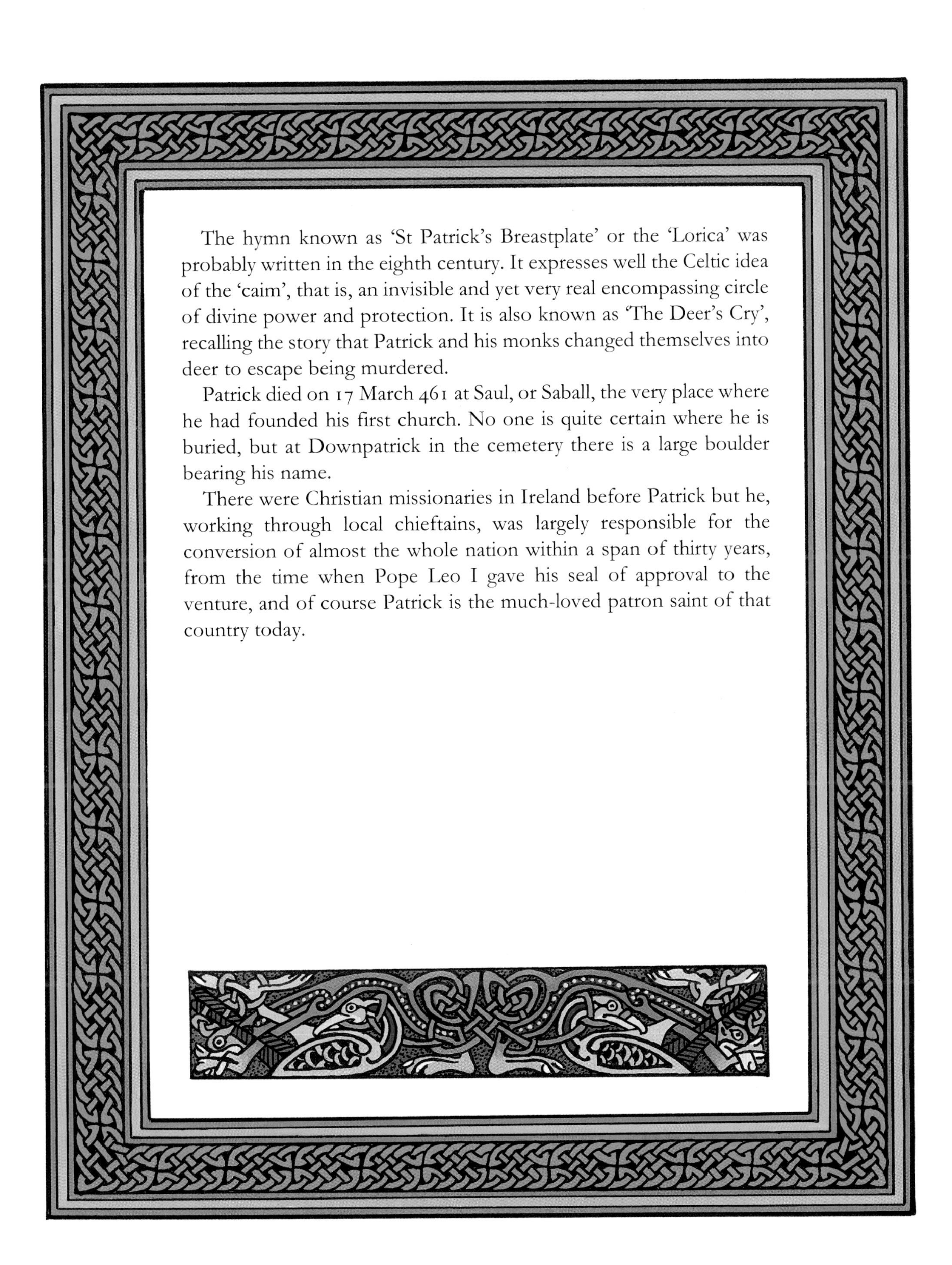

The hymn known as 'St Patrick's Breastplate' or the 'Lorica' was probably written in the eighth century. It expresses well the Celtic idea of the 'caim', that is, an invisible and yet very real encompassing circle of divine power and protection. It is also known as 'The Deer's Cry', recalling the story that Patrick and his monks changed themselves into deer to escape being murdered.

Patrick died on 17 March 461 at Saul, or Saball, the very place where he had founded his first church. No one is quite certain where he is buried, but at Downpatrick in the cemetery there is a large boulder bearing his name.

There were Christian missionaries in Ireland before Patrick but he, working through local chieftains, was largely responsible for the conversion of almost the whole nation within a span of thirty years, from the time when Pope Leo I gave his seal of approval to the venture, and of course Patrick is the much-loved patron saint of that country today.

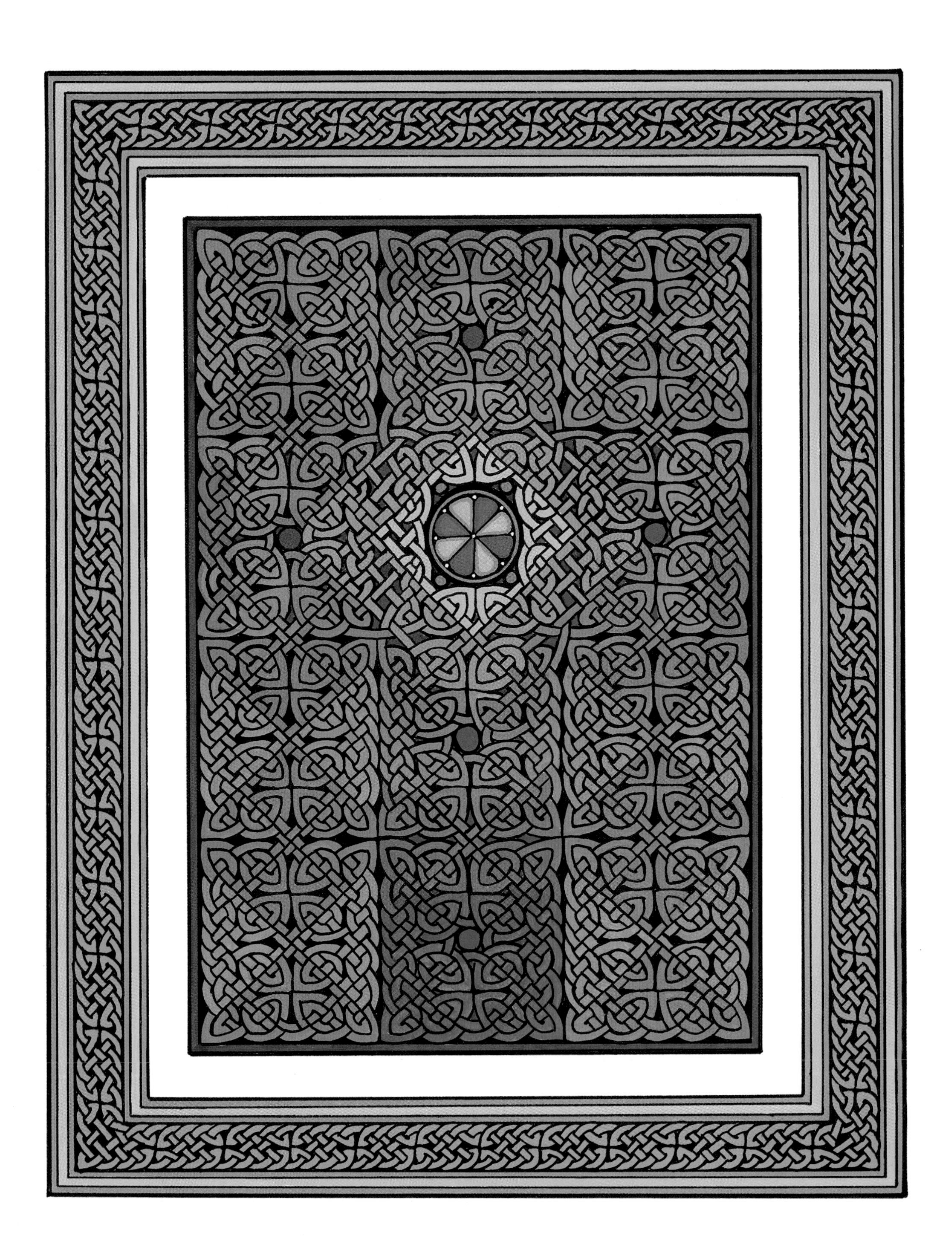

Aidan

FEAST DAY: 31 August

In the summer of AD 635 an Irish monk arrived in Northumbria from Iona at the invitation of the Christian King Oswald. He was related to St Bridget and during his early life had spent some time in the community on Scattery Island in County Clare. Apart from these scant details nothing much is known of his origins.

King Oswald himself had been educated by the monks on Iona, but his people were still largely pagan. Initially he had invited Corman, but due to the harsh and unbending manner of that particular monk the mission had failed – after a few months he had gone home, complaining that the Northumbrians were stubborn, barbarous and uncivilized, and declaring the task impossible.

By common consent and under

Lord, this bare island, make it thy place of peace.
Here be the peace of brothers serving men.
Here be the peace of holy rules obeying.
Here be the peace of praise by dark or day.
Be this island thy holy island.
I, Lord, thy servant Aidan, speak this prayer.
Be it in thy care. Amen.

A prayer attributed to St Aidan and still used daily on Lindisfarne

the authority of the abbot Seghen, Aidan was chosen for the task and duly consecrated bishop. As a centre for his missionary activity St Aidan chose the island of Lindisfarne rather than the vacant see of York. Perhaps it reminded him of Iona, or perhaps he felt that York was too much influenced by the church of Rome, from which the British church was still quite separate. Certainly it was conveniently near and in view of the royal castle at Bamburgh, where Oswald lived. Aidan and Oswald often travelled together teaching and preaching, for at first Aidan spoke only his native Irish and Oswald, who had knowledge of both languages, had to translate the saint's words into English so that the people could understand them.

Aidan lived a frugal life, but one year he joined King Oswald for his Easter feast, where many splendid foods were set out on dishes of solid silver. Just as grace was about to be said, one of the stewards hurried in to report that there was a rabble of destitute people, hungry and noisy, pressing at the gate asking for food. Oswald commanded that the spread should be taken and distributed among them, and that when they had eaten the silver dishes should be broken up and given to them as well. Aidan, of course, was delighted at the King's generosity and grabbed his hand, declaring, 'May this hand never perish.' Strangely enough, the Venerable Bede tells us that after his death Oswald's hand was indeed preserved in a silver casket at Bamburgh.

Following the example of the Irish monastic system, with which he was familiar, Aidan started a school for English boys, partly so that the church would not have to rely on a supply of priests from Ireland or Scotland and could eventually become independent. Among his first pupils were some well-known saints of the Celtic church such as Eata and Boisil of Melrose, Wilfrid of Hexham and the brothers Cedd of Tilbury and Chad of Lichfield.

It was a custom among both the Saxons and the Celts to sell their children into slavery, and whenever he could Aidan would redeem and educate these children, using any resources that were given to him as

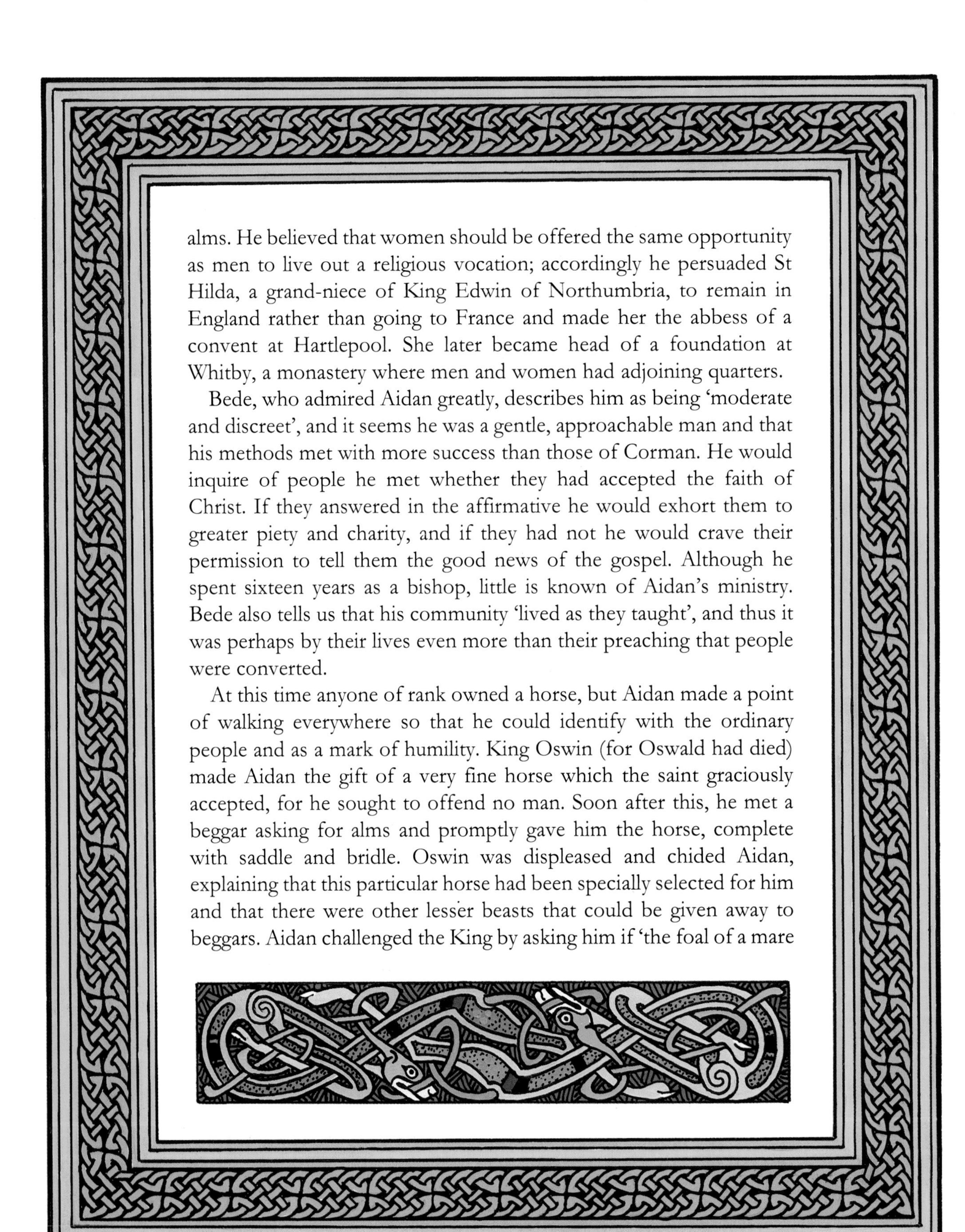

alms. He believed that women should be offered the same opportunity as men to live out a religious vocation; accordingly he persuaded St Hilda, a grand-niece of King Edwin of Northumbria, to remain in England rather than going to France and made her the abbess of a convent at Hartlepool. She later became head of a foundation at Whitby, a monastery where men and women had adjoining quarters.

Bede, who admired Aidan greatly, describes him as being 'moderate and discreet', and it seems he was a gentle, approachable man and that his methods met with more success than those of Corman. He would inquire of people he met whether they had accepted the faith of Christ. If they answered in the affirmative he would exhort them to greater piety and charity, and if they had not he would crave their permission to tell them the good news of the gospel. Although he spent sixteen years as a bishop, little is known of Aidan's ministry. Bede also tells us that his community 'lived as they taught', and thus it was perhaps by their lives even more than their preaching that people were converted.

At this time anyone of rank owned a horse, but Aidan made a point of walking everywhere so that he could identify with the ordinary people and as a mark of humility. King Oswin (for Oswald had died) made Aidan the gift of a very fine horse which the saint graciously accepted, for he sought to offend no man. Soon after this, he met a beggar asking for alms and promptly gave him the horse, complete with saddle and bridle. Oswin was displeased and chided Aidan, explaining that this particular horse had been specially selected for him and that there were other lesser beasts that could be given away to beggars. Aidan challenged the King by asking him if 'the foal of a mare

was more important than a beggar, the child of God'. After some thought Oswin concurred and sought forgiveness.

Like most of the Celtic saints, it was Aidan's habit to withdraw at intervals to a solitary place for prayer. For this purpose he used Inner Farne, the island where Cuthbert was later to spend much of his life. It was from here that he witnessed the royal residence of Bamburgh being devoured by flames, for the enemy king, Penda of Mercia, had pulled down surrounding houses and barns for fuel, piled the wood and thatch around the base of the stronghold and waited for a favourable wind before setting fire to it all. Due to Aidan's timely intervention, the direction of the wind quickly changed and the Northumbrians were saved. Bede mentions not only the saint's power over natural forces, but also his ability to foretell the future. Both these gifts are illustrated by the following story.

A priest named Utta was commissioned by King Oswy to escort his future queen, Eanfleda, from Kent, where she had taken refuge with her widowed mother and the bishop Paulinus after her father, Edwin, had been killed by the same Penda. She was Oswy's cousin and a Christian. It was arranged that the priest should travel to Kent by land and return by sea. Before setting out he went to Aidan for a blessing

and the saint gave Utta a flask of oil, telling him that he would encounter a great storm on his homeward journey and that he was to pour the contents on the sea, by which it would be stilled. And Bede tells us that it was so.

St Aidan also foresaw the imminent death of his dear friend and benefactor King Oswin. The kingdom of Bernicia, consisting of present-day Northumberland and part of south-east Scotland, was ruled by Oswy. Deira to the south, now North Yorkshire and County Durham, had Oswin as its king. Oswy wanted to rule the whole of this territory and so raised an army to attack Oswin, who fled to a supposed friend, by whom he was betrayed. His subsequent murder must have distressed Aidan deeply and caused him much sadness, for he regarded both reputedly Christian kings as his friends but he had been especially close to Oswin. It has been suggested that this event actually hastened his own death, for it was only twelve days later that he was taken ill and died, on 31 August 651. A makeshift tent had been erected for him against the west wall of the church, and he expired while leaning his head against one of the posts that strengthened the outer wall. A later wooden church on this site caught fire and burned

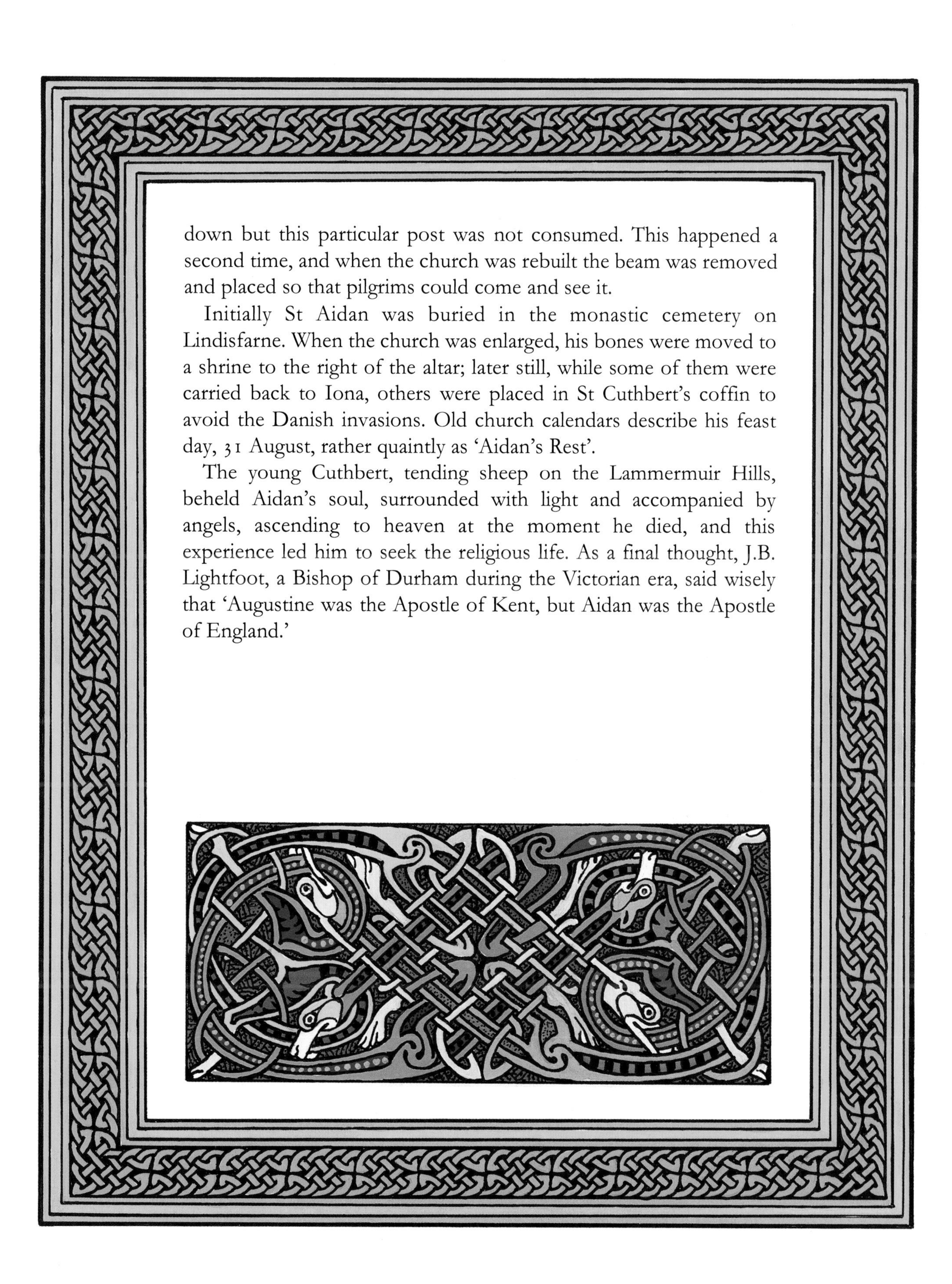

down but this particular post was not consumed. This happened a second time, and when the church was rebuilt the beam was removed and placed so that pilgrims could come and see it.

Initially St Aidan was buried in the monastic cemetery on Lindisfarne. When the church was enlarged, his bones were moved to a shrine to the right of the altar; later still, while some of them were carried back to Iona, others were placed in St Cuthbert's coffin to avoid the Danish invasions. Old church calendars describe his feast day, 31 August, rather quaintly as 'Aidan's Rest'.

The young Cuthbert, tending sheep on the Lammermuir Hills, beheld Aidan's soul, surrounded with light and accompanied by angels, ascending to heaven at the moment he died, and this experience led him to seek the religious life. As a final thought, J.B. Lightfoot, a Bishop of Durham during the Victorian era, said wisely that 'Augustine was the Apostle of Kent, but Aidan was the Apostle of England.'

David

FEAST DAY: 1 March

Today the small city of St David's seems to be a remote and isolated settlement, but during the Age of the Saints the western sea-routes linking Scotland, Ireland, Wales, Cornwall and Brittany with continental Europe were much used for trade and cultural exchange, and communication was excellent. It is from this wild and windswept part of West Wales that the patron saint of that country comes: St David, or Dewi Sant as he is known by the Welsh.

David's birth, the date of which is uncertain, was foretold by an angel thirty years before it happened, first to his father Sant, of the royal house of Ceredigion, and then to St Patrick. Sant, for whom David was named, heard in a dream an angel voice which told him that on his hunting

. . . Dewi's huts
Of daub and wattle, rigour
Of cold water, bread, and herbs.
Ascetic missionary,
He broke, yoke across shoulders,
Ground hard as the human heart,
Struck from the rock of this dell
A well of living water
To christen the soil of Wales.

From 'At St David's' by
Joseph P. Clancy

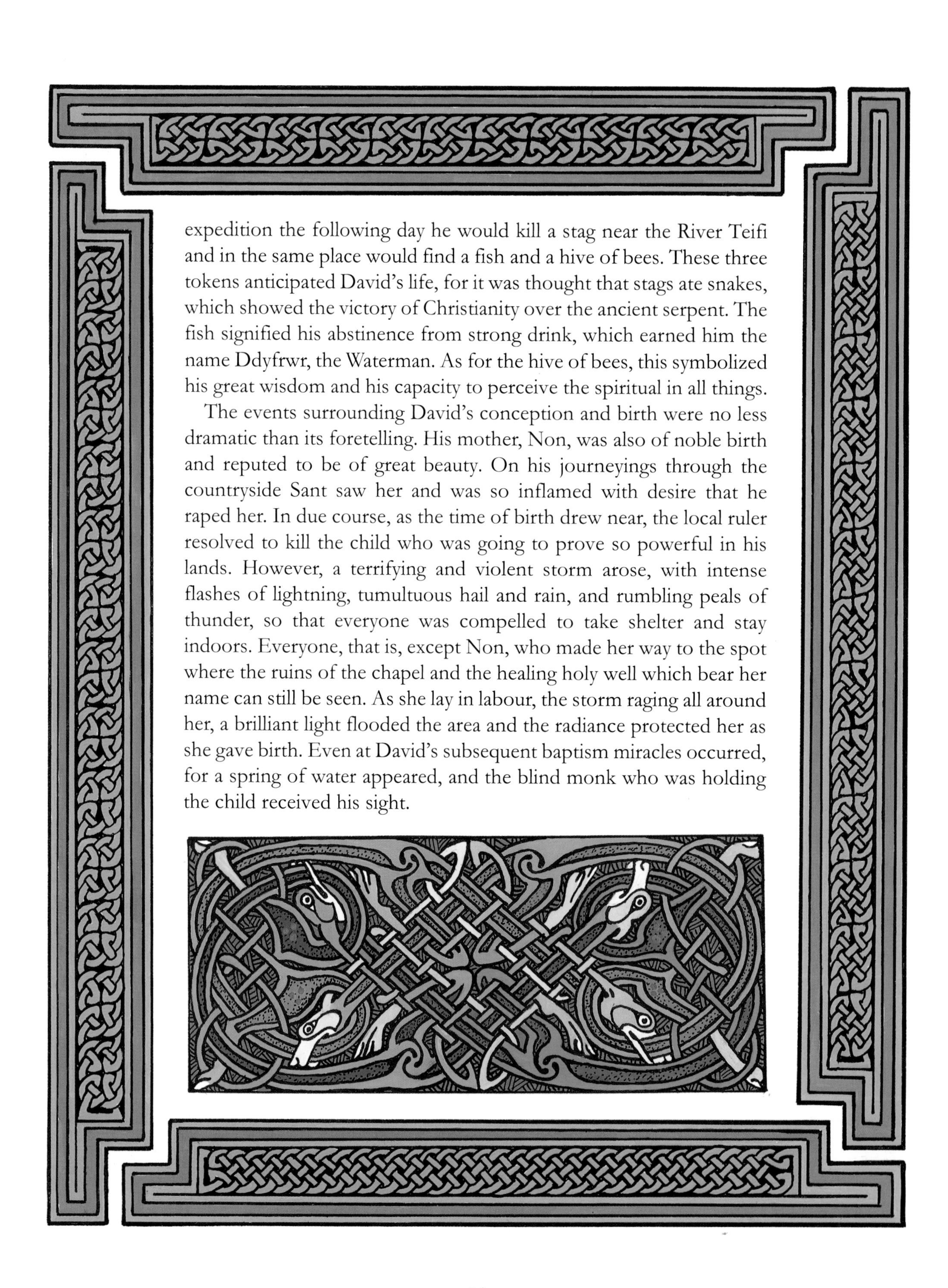

expedition the following day he would kill a stag near the River Teifi and in the same place would find a fish and a hive of bees. These three tokens anticipated David's life, for it was thought that stags ate snakes, which showed the victory of Christianity over the ancient serpent. The fish signified his abstinence from strong drink, which earned him the name Ddyfrwr, the Waterman. As for the hive of bees, this symbolized his great wisdom and his capacity to perceive the spiritual in all things.

The events surrounding David's conception and birth were no less dramatic than its foretelling. His mother, Non, was also of noble birth and reputed to be of great beauty. On his journeyings through the countryside Sant saw her and was so inflamed with desire that he raped her. In due course, as the time of birth drew near, the local ruler resolved to kill the child who was going to prove so powerful in his lands. However, a terrifying and violent storm arose, with intense flashes of lightning, tumultuous hail and rain, and rumbling peals of thunder, so that everyone was compelled to take shelter and stay indoors. Everyone, that is, except Non, who made her way to the spot where the ruins of the chapel and the healing holy well which bear her name can still be seen. As she lay in labour, the storm raging all around her, a brilliant light flooded the area and the radiance protected her as she gave birth. Even at David's subsequent baptism miracles occurred, for a spring of water appeared, and the blind monk who was holding the child received his sight.

David was educated to the priesthood at the Celtic monastery of Henfynyw, where his companions would see a golden-beaked pigeon playing at his lips and teaching him, singing with him. Later he undertook missionary journeys to various places including Glastonbury, and then returned to found his own monastery at Glyn Rhosin. It was an austere life, following the example of the Desert Fathers, but one embraced with a willing heart. The monks ploughed without oxen, using their own bodies to pull the plough. They took little sustenance, mainly bread, herbs, salt and water, observed silence unless it was necessary to speak, and had no personal possessions. Long hours were spent in prayer and praise.

When the Synod of Llanddewi Brefi took place, because of the large crowds none of the bishops could make themselves heard despite standing on a great heap of garments. Eventually, after much persuasion, David agreed to come and, laying a small cloth on the ground, he stood on it. At once the ground rose up to form

a hill, from which he addressed the people. As he spoke, a white dove descended and stayed on his shoulder. Today statues and stained-glass images of the saint often show him with this dove, said to represent his eloquence.

During his life David undertook a pilgrimage to Jerusalem, where he was consecrated as a bishop (some say archbishop) by the Patriarch John III, who gave him gifts of a staff, a bell, a golden tunic, and a portable altar. This altar may still be seen today in the south transept of the cathedral. Also in the cathedral, in the Holy Trinity Chapel behind the high altar, is the shrine containing David's relics. People still make pilgrimages to this holy place as they did in medieval times, for Dewi Sant of Menevia is even now a light and inspiration to many.

Michael

FEAST DAY: 29 September

Then war broke out in heaven. Michael and his angels waged war upon the dragon. The dragon and his angels fought, but they had not the strength to win, and no foothold was left them in heaven.

The Book of Revelation, chapter 12, verse 7

Angelic visions and visitations often played a significant part in the lives of the Celtic saints. For the Celt, both pagan and Christian, perception of the next world overlapped strongly with the awareness of this one. Death was only a door between the worlds and the veil was very thin indeed, especially at certain times of the year and in particular places. Angels, as messengers, formed a link between the visible and invisible worlds; they became a bridge between spirit and matter.

The chief archangel, Michael, is much beloved of the Celtic peoples, and there are many dedications to him in Christian places of worship and also in topographical features. Important Michael sites are usually on

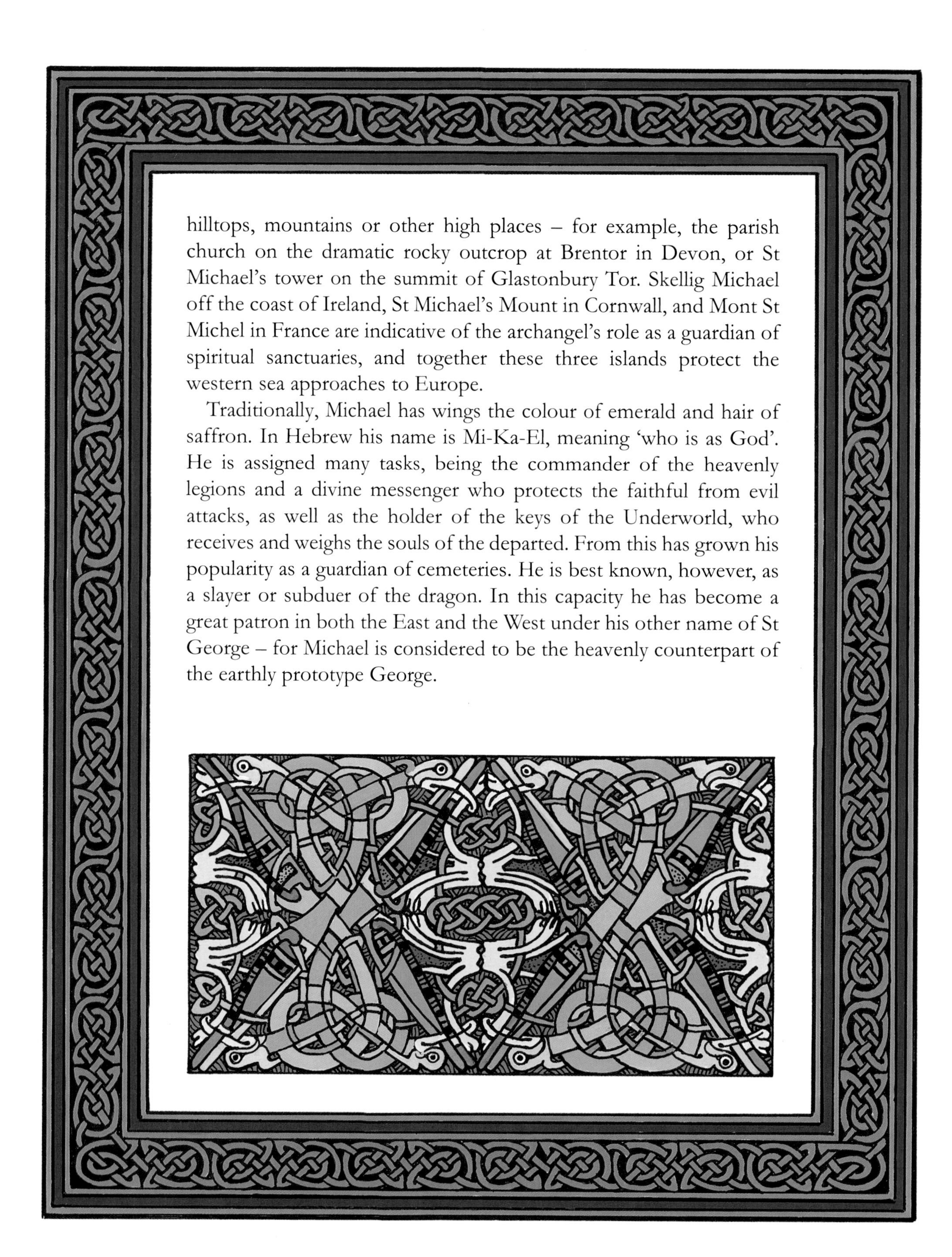

hilltops, mountains or other high places – for example, the parish church on the dramatic rocky outcrop at Brentor in Devon, or St Michael's tower on the summit of Glastonbury Tor. Skellig Michael off the coast of Ireland, St Michael's Mount in Cornwall, and Mont St Michel in France are indicative of the archangel's role as a guardian of spiritual sanctuaries, and together these three islands protect the western sea approaches to Europe.

Traditionally, Michael has wings the colour of emerald and hair of saffron. In Hebrew his name is Mi-Ka-El, meaning 'who is as God'. He is assigned many tasks, being the commander of the heavenly legions and a divine messenger who protects the faithful from evil attacks, as well as the holder of the keys of the Underworld, who receives and weighs the souls of the departed. From this has grown his popularity as a guardian of cemeteries. He is best known, however, as a slayer or subduer of the dragon. In this capacity he has become a great patron in both the East and the West under his other name of St George – for Michael is considered to be the heavenly counterpart of the earthly prototype George.

From early times his cult was strong in the British Isles, and the Venerable Bede mentions an oratory and a cemetery near Hexham dedicated to him. Cornwall is under the guardianship of Michael or Sen Myghal. He appeared to some fishermen standing in shining glory on a western promontory of St Michael's Mount, now known as 'St Michael's Chair' or 'Cadar Myghal'. He is said to have 'healed their eyes', that is, opened their vision. This occurred on 8 May in AD 495, and this day in the year is when the town of Helston remembers its patron Michael, with its Flora Day. Part of the day's festivities include the 'Hal an Tow', a pageant in which the victory of St George over the dragon is re-enacted in the streets. A similar apparition is also said to have taken place at Mont St Michel.

One of the recently discovered Dead Sea Scrolls is entitled 'War of the Sons of Light Against the Sons of Darkness'. Here Michael is called the 'Prince of Light', and he leads his angels in battle against the legions of darkness.

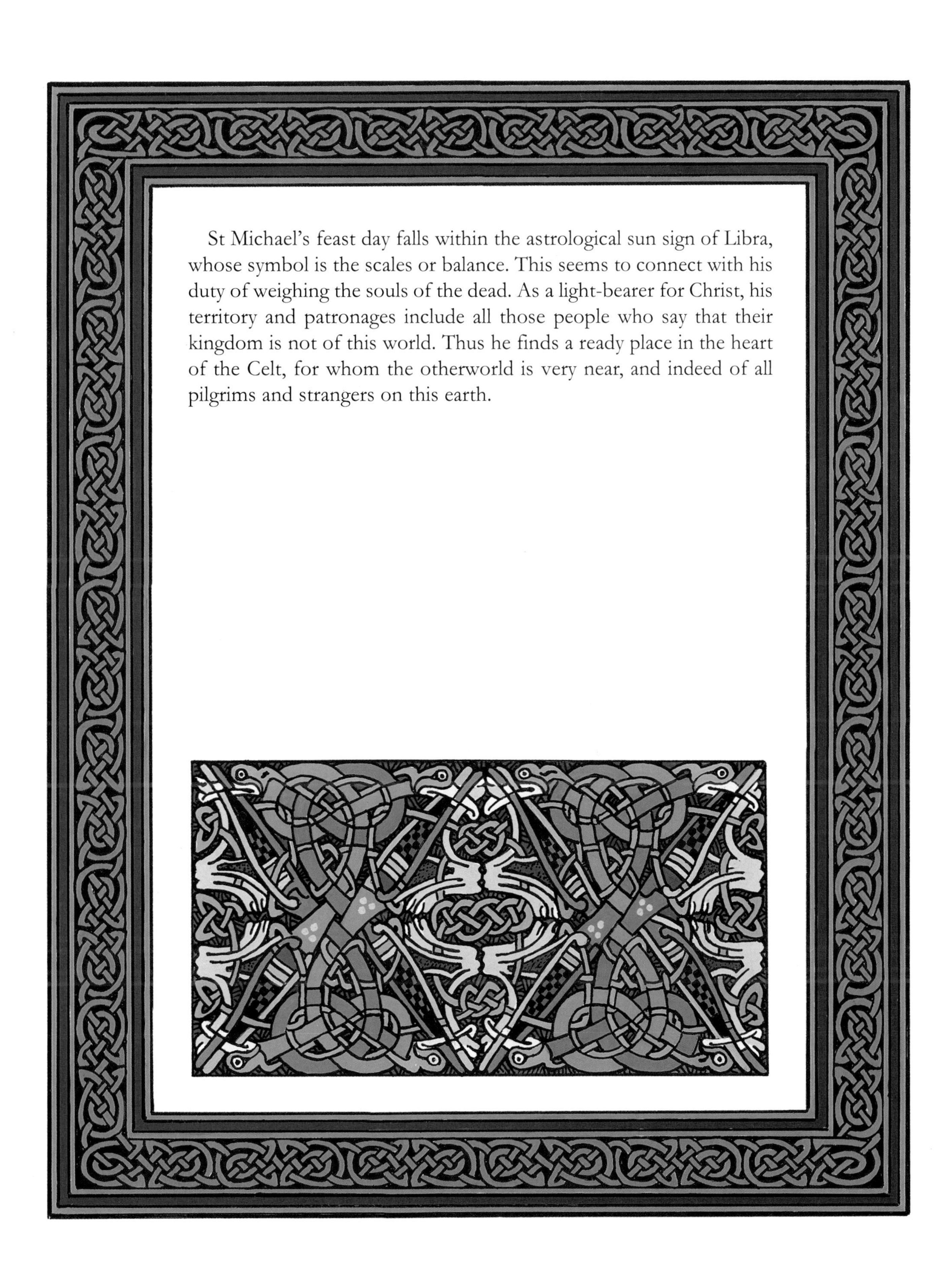

St Michael's feast day falls within the astrological sun sign of Libra, whose symbol is the scales or balance. This seems to connect with his duty of weighing the souls of the dead. As a light-bearer for Christ, his territory and patronages include all those people who say that their kingdom is not of this world. Thus he finds a ready place in the heart of the Celt, for whom the otherworld is very near, and indeed of all pilgrims and strangers on this earth.

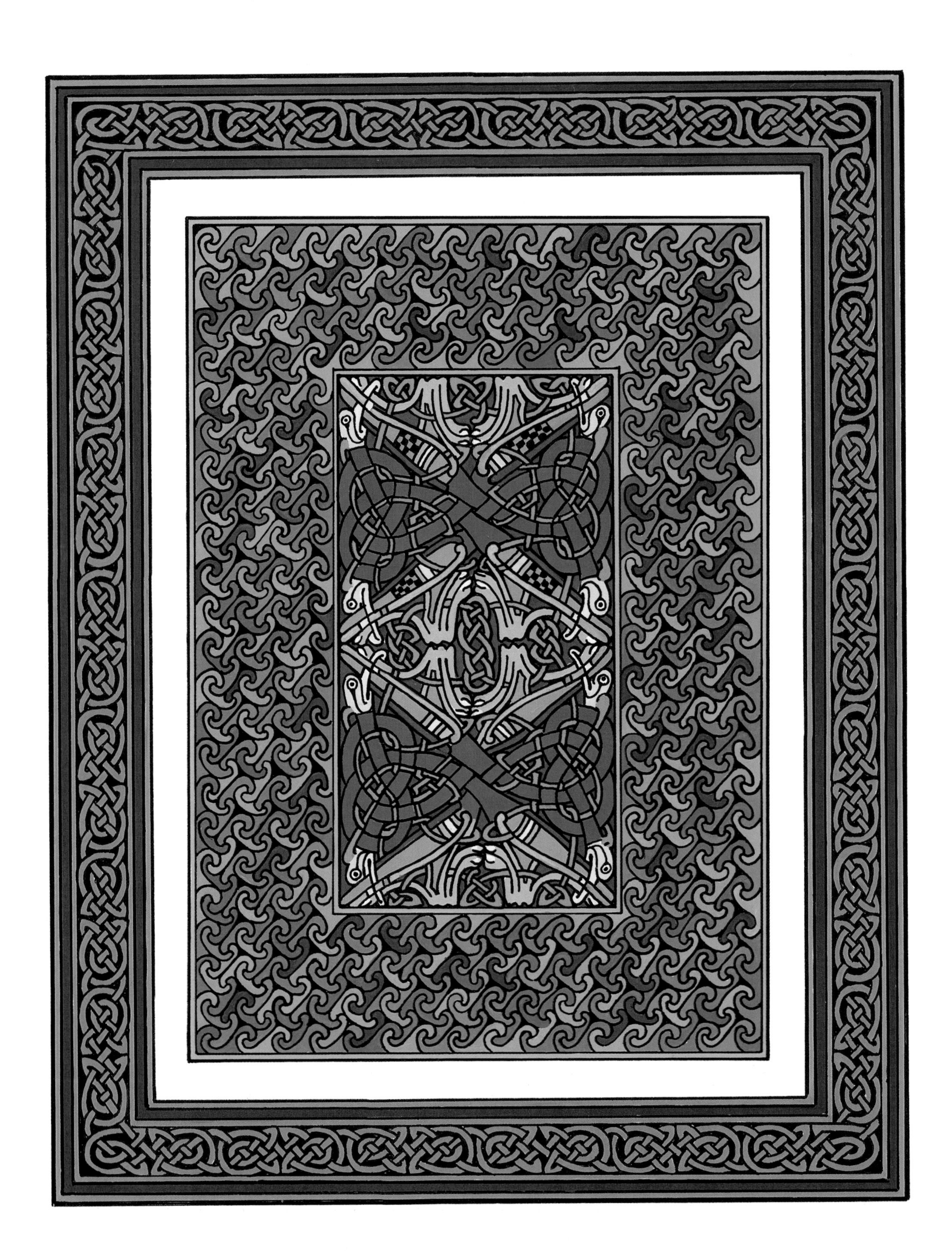

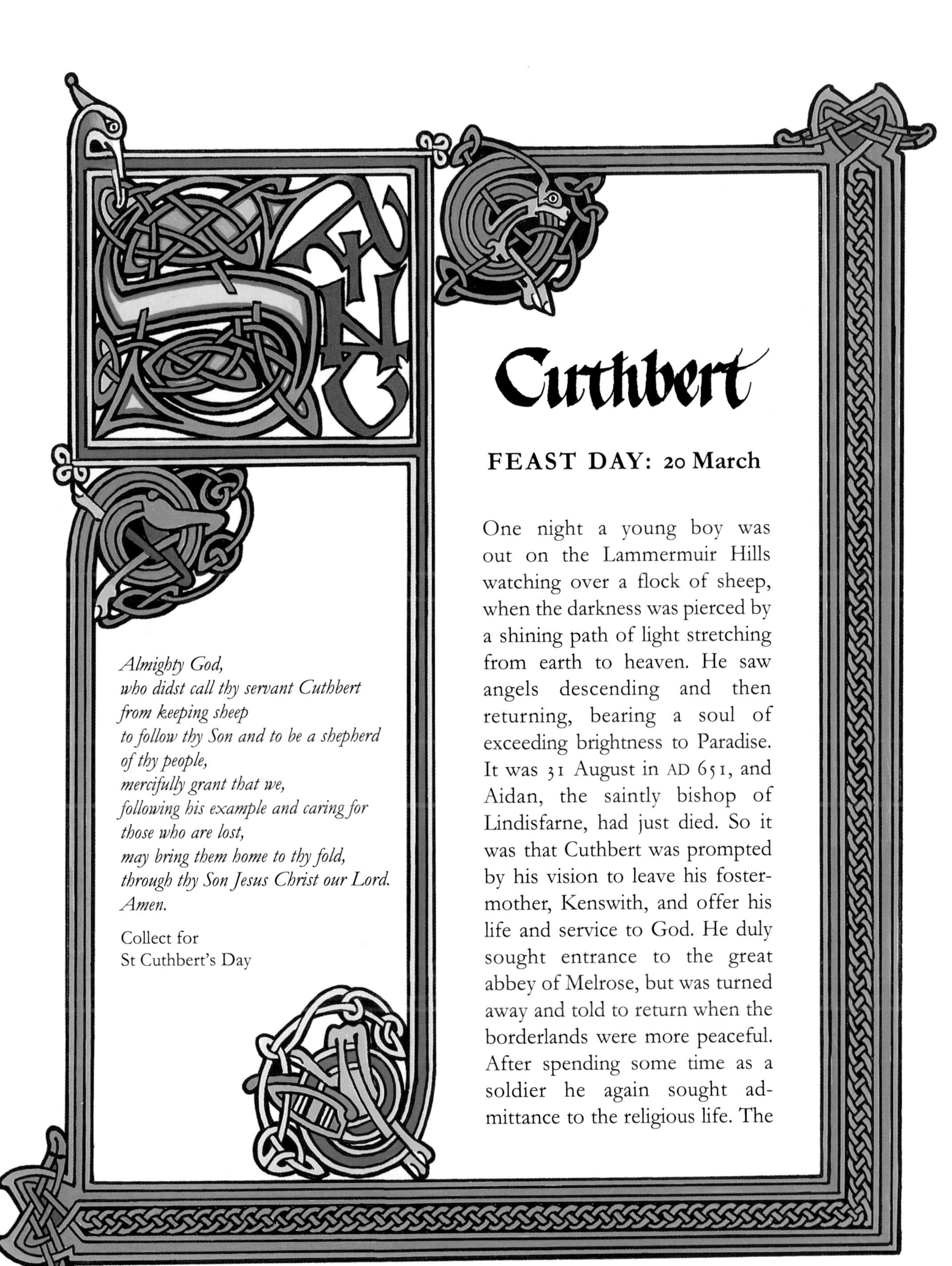

Cuthbert

FEAST DAY: 20 March

One night a young boy was out on the Lammermuir Hills watching over a flock of sheep, when the darkness was pierced by a shining path of light stretching from earth to heaven. He saw angels descending and then returning, bearing a soul of exceeding brightness to Paradise. It was 31 August in AD 651, and Aidan, the saintly bishop of Lindisfarne, had just died. So it was that Cuthbert was prompted by his vision to leave his foster-mother, Kenswith, and offer his life and service to God. He duly sought entrance to the great abbey of Melrose, but was turned away and told to return when the borderlands were more peaceful. After spending some time as a soldier he again sought admittance to the religious life. The

Almighty God,
who didst call thy servant Cuthbert
from keeping sheep
to follow thy Son and to be a shepherd
of thy people,
mercifully grant that we,
following his example and caring for
those who are lost,
may bring them home to thy fold,
through thy Son Jesus Christ our Lord.
Amen.

Collect for
St Cuthbert's Day

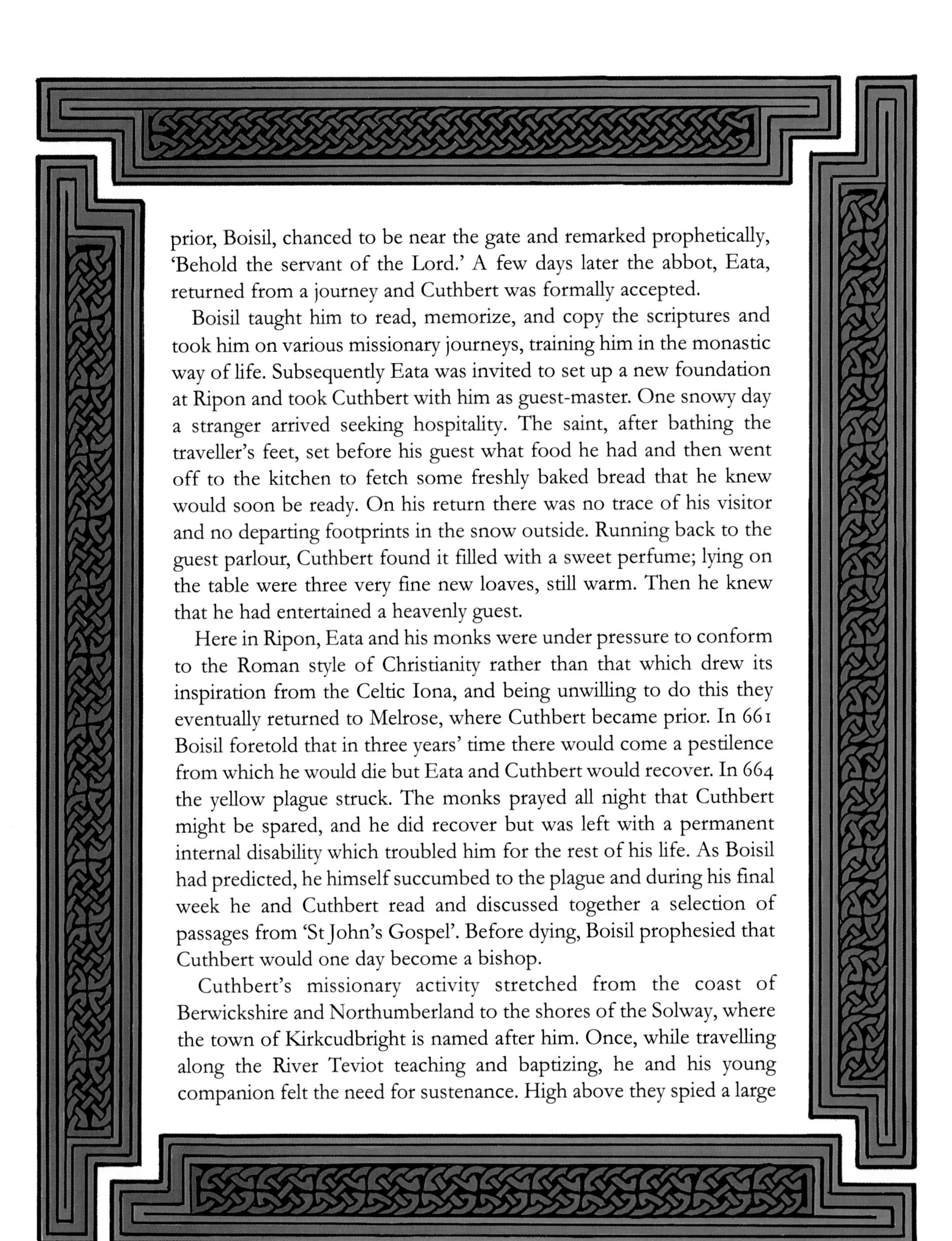

prior, Boisil, chanced to be near the gate and remarked prophetically, 'Behold the servant of the Lord.' A few days later the abbot, Eata, returned from a journey and Cuthbert was formally accepted.

Boisil taught him to read, memorize, and copy the scriptures and took him on various missionary journeys, training him in the monastic way of life. Subsequently Eata was invited to set up a new foundation at Ripon and took Cuthbert with him as guest-master. One snowy day a stranger arrived seeking hospitality. The saint, after bathing the traveller's feet, set before his guest what food he had and then went off to the kitchen to fetch some freshly baked bread that he knew would soon be ready. On his return there was no trace of his visitor and no departing footprints in the snow outside. Running back to the guest parlour, Cuthbert found it filled with a sweet perfume; lying on the table were three very fine new loaves, still warm. Then he knew that he had entertained a heavenly guest.

Here in Ripon, Eata and his monks were under pressure to conform to the Roman style of Christianity rather than that which drew its inspiration from the Celtic Iona, and being unwilling to do this they eventually returned to Melrose, where Cuthbert became prior. In 661 Boisil foretold that in three years' time there would come a pestilence from which he would die but Eata and Cuthbert would recover. In 664 the yellow plague struck. The monks prayed all night that Cuthbert might be spared, and he did recover but was left with a permanent internal disability which troubled him for the rest of his life. As Boisil had predicted, he himself succumbed to the plague and during his final week he and Cuthbert read and discussed together a selection of passages from 'St John's Gospel'. Before dying, Boisil prophesied that Cuthbert would one day become a bishop.

Cuthbert's missionary activity stretched from the coast of Berwickshire and Northumberland to the shores of the Solway, where the town of Kirkcudbright is named after him. Once, while travelling along the River Teviot teaching and baptizing, he and his young companion felt the need for sustenance. High above they spied a large

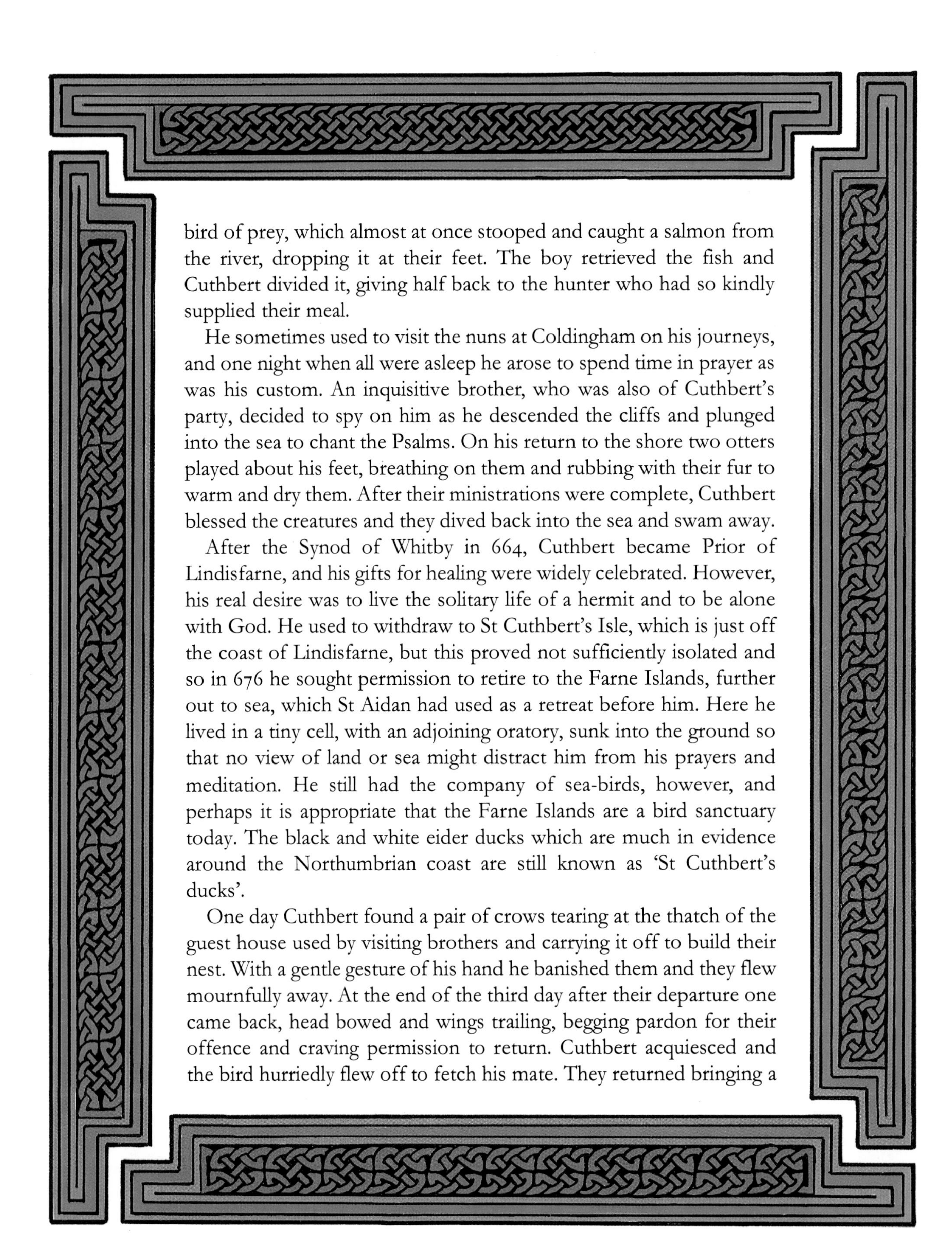

bird of prey, which almost at once stooped and caught a salmon from the river, dropping it at their feet. The boy retrieved the fish and Cuthbert divided it, giving half back to the hunter who had so kindly supplied their meal.

He sometimes used to visit the nuns at Coldingham on his journeys, and one night when all were asleep he arose to spend time in prayer as was his custom. An inquisitive brother, who was also of Cuthbert's party, decided to spy on him as he descended the cliffs and plunged into the sea to chant the Psalms. On his return to the shore two otters played about his feet, breathing on them and rubbing with their fur to warm and dry them. After their ministrations were complete, Cuthbert blessed the creatures and they dived back into the sea and swam away.

After the Synod of Whitby in 664, Cuthbert became Prior of Lindisfarne, and his gifts for healing were widely celebrated. However, his real desire was to live the solitary life of a hermit and to be alone with God. He used to withdraw to St Cuthbert's Isle, which is just off the coast of Lindisfarne, but this proved not sufficiently isolated and so in 676 he sought permission to retire to the Farne Islands, further out to sea, which St Aidan had used as a retreat before him. Here he lived in a tiny cell, with an adjoining oratory, sunk into the ground so that no view of land or sea might distract him from his prayers and meditation. He still had the company of sea-birds, however, and perhaps it is appropriate that the Farne Islands are a bird sanctuary today. The black and white eider ducks which are much in evidence around the Northumbrian coast are still known as 'St Cuthbert's ducks'.

One day Cuthbert found a pair of crows tearing at the thatch of the guest house used by visiting brothers and carrying it off to build their nest. With a gentle gesture of his hand he banished them and they flew mournfully away. At the end of the third day after their departure one came back, head bowed and wings trailing, begging pardon for their offence and craving permission to return. Cuthbert acquiesced and the bird hurriedly flew off to fetch his mate. They returned bringing a

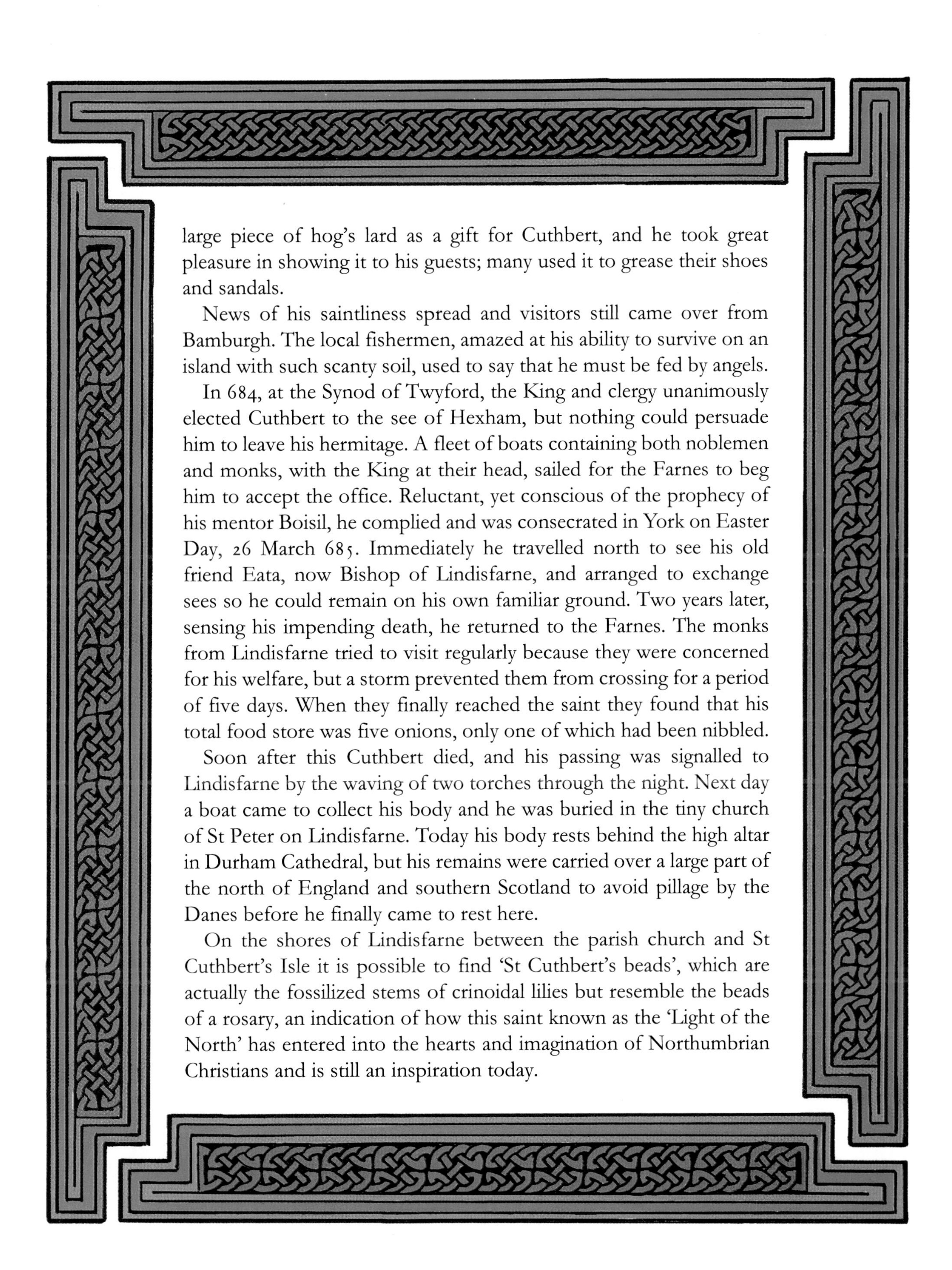

large piece of hog's lard as a gift for Cuthbert, and he took great pleasure in showing it to his guests; many used it to grease their shoes and sandals.

News of his saintliness spread and visitors still came over from Bamburgh. The local fishermen, amazed at his ability to survive on an island with such scanty soil, used to say that he must be fed by angels.

In 684, at the Synod of Twyford, the King and clergy unanimously elected Cuthbert to the see of Hexham, but nothing could persuade him to leave his hermitage. A fleet of boats containing both noblemen and monks, with the King at their head, sailed for the Farnes to beg him to accept the office. Reluctant, yet conscious of the prophecy of his mentor Boisil, he complied and was consecrated in York on Easter Day, 26 March 685. Immediately he travelled north to see his old friend Eata, now Bishop of Lindisfarne, and arranged to exchange sees so he could remain on his own familiar ground. Two years later, sensing his impending death, he returned to the Farnes. The monks from Lindisfarne tried to visit regularly because they were concerned for his welfare, but a storm prevented them from crossing for a period of five days. When they finally reached the saint they found that his total food store was five onions, only one of which had been nibbled.

Soon after this Cuthbert died, and his passing was signalled to Lindisfarne by the waving of two torches through the night. Next day a boat came to collect his body and he was buried in the tiny church of St Peter on Lindisfarne. Today his body rests behind the high altar in Durham Cathedral, but his remains were carried over a large part of the north of England and southern Scotland to avoid pillage by the Danes before he finally came to rest here.

On the shores of Lindisfarne between the parish church and St Cuthbert's Isle it is possible to find 'St Cuthbert's beads', which are actually the fossilized stems of crinoidal lilies but resemble the beads of a rosary, an indication of how this saint known as the 'Light of the North' has entered into the hearts and imagination of Northumbrian Christians and is still an inspiration today.

St Winefride

FEAST DAY: 3 November

Here to this holy well shall
pilgrimages be,
And not from purple Wales only nor
from elmy England,
But from beyond seas, Erin, France
and Flanders, everywhere,
Pilgrims, still pilgrims, more pilgrims,
still more poor pilgrims.

From 'St Winefred's Well' by
Gerard Manley Hopkins

The healing waters of St Winefride's well at Treffynnon, or Holywell, in North Wales have been visited down the ages by royal personages and more humble pilgrims alike. It is the only shrine in the British Isles to have withstood the destruction of the Reformation and to have remained consistently as a place of pilgrimage. At present it is open throughout the year from morning until dusk, and traditionally visitors pass through the water three times. The origin of this custom may derive from the ancient Celtic rite of baptism by triple immersion.

But what of St Winefride, or Gwenfrewi as she is known in Welsh, after whom the site is named? Like many of the Celtic saints she was of noble birth,

being the virgin daughter of a local prince, Tefydd, and his wife, Gwenlo. Caradog, from nearby Hawarden and also of royal blood, was pursuing her for his own ends, and in her terror Winefride fled to the safety of the church. Before she could gain sanctuary Caradog caught up with her at the church door, and in his fury at being refused he beheaded her. Her body lay outside the building while her head fell inside. Immediately a spring rose up on the spot where her severed head lay, and this was the source of the holy well. The legend goes on to tell how St Beuno, Winefride's uncle, placed her head next to her body and prayed that she might be restored to life. Winefride was made whole and arose with only a white scar around her neck to testify to her martyrdom, while Caradog was swallowed up by the earth and never seen again.

There is a touching story of how Beuno requested his niece to send him a woollen cloak each year on the feast day of St John the Baptist,

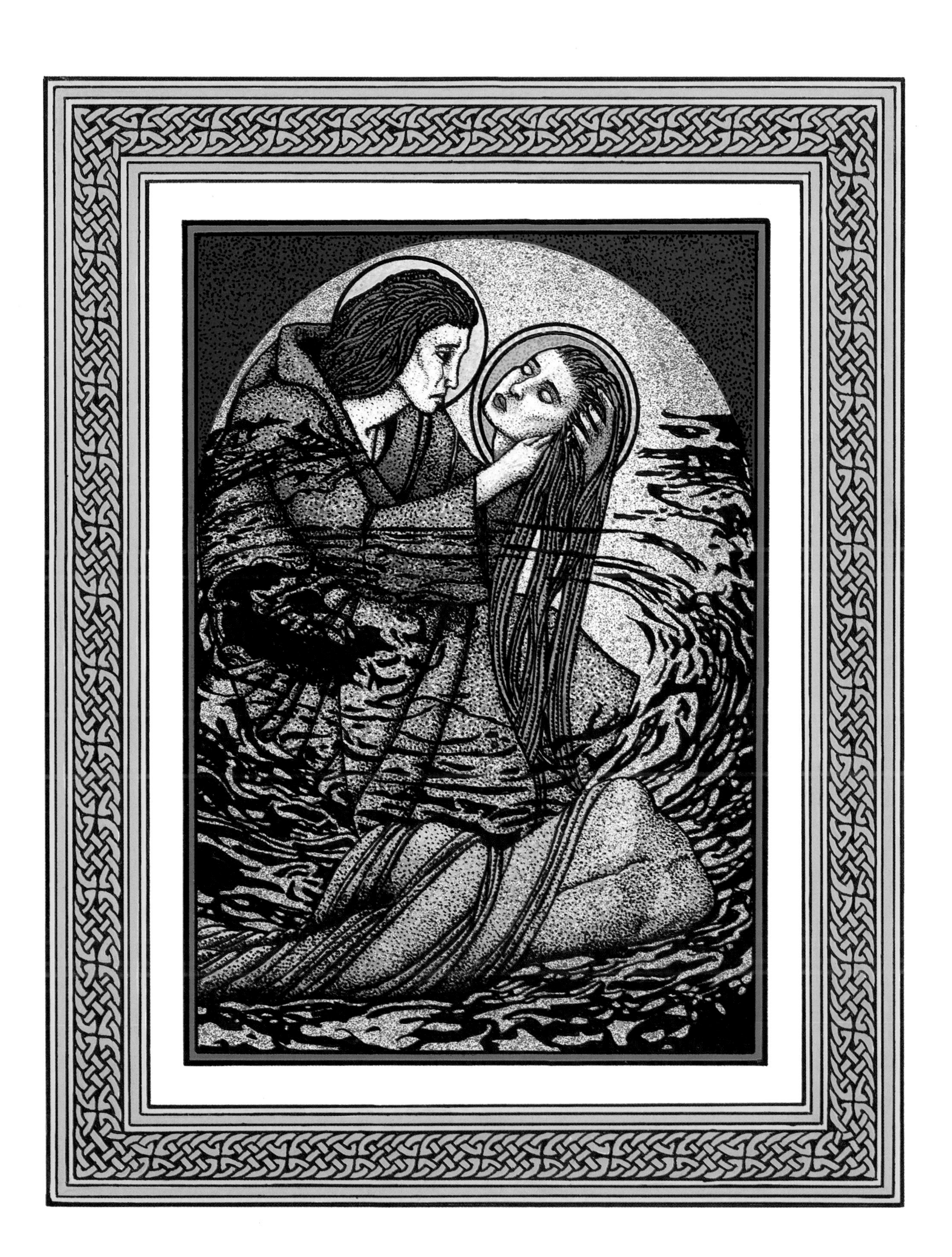

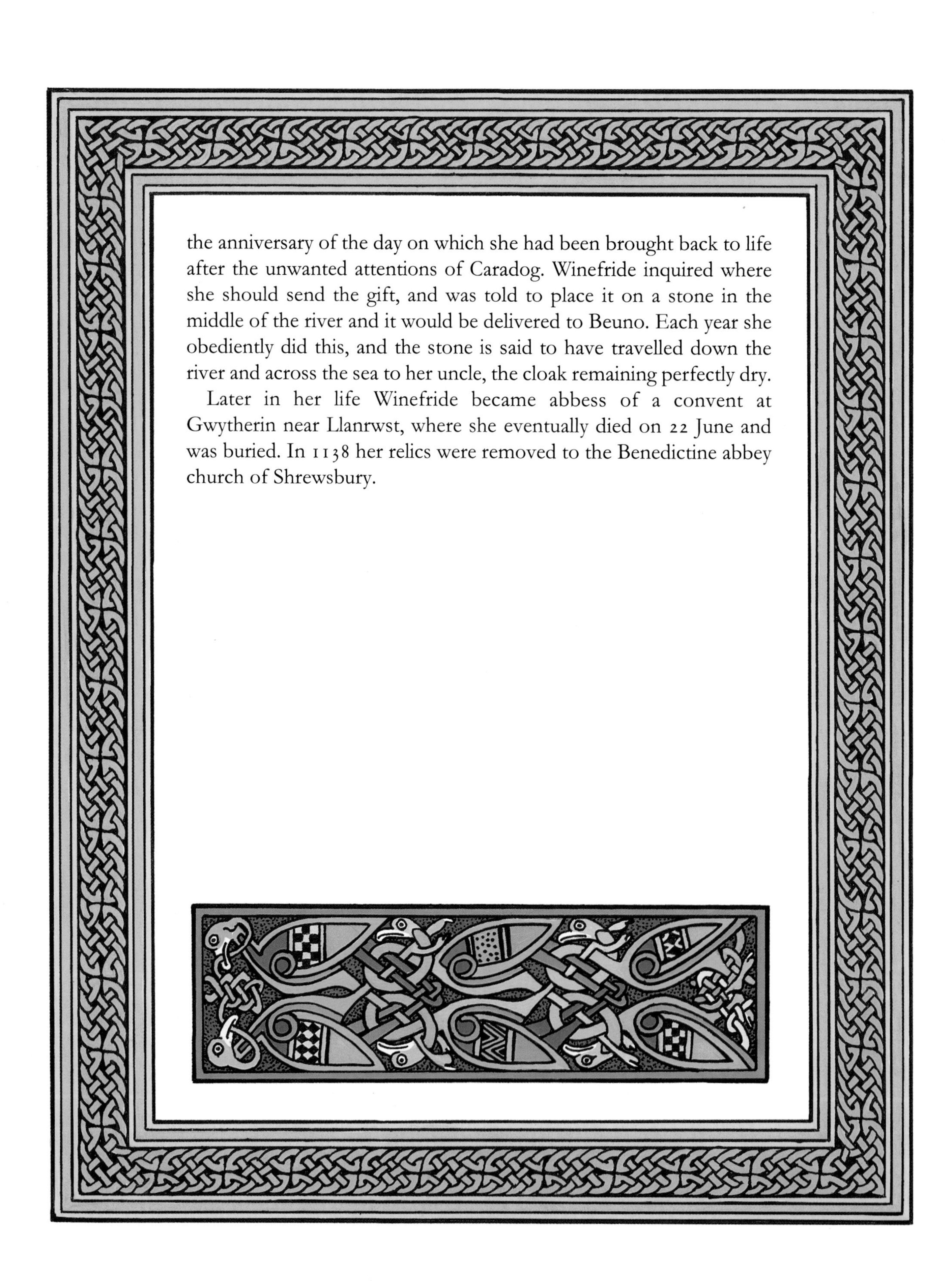

the anniversary of the day on which she had been brought back to life after the unwanted attentions of Caradog. Winefride inquired where she should send the gift, and was told to place it on a stone in the middle of the river and it would be delivered to Beuno. Each year she obediently did this, and the stone is said to have travelled down the river and across the sea to her uncle, the cloak remaining perfectly dry.

Later in her life Winefride became abbess of a convent at Gwytherin near Llanrwst, where she eventually died on 22 June and was buried. In 1138 her relics were removed to the Benedictine abbey church of Shrewsbury.

Kentigern

FEAST DAY: 13 January

I see the chosen missionaries go
from Mungo's burning centre, to and fro.
North into Shetland and the Orkneys, North
even to Norway, living for Christ's sake
and planted there grow churches in their wake.

from *The Hidden Stream*
by Dorothy S. Walton

Loth, a British chieftain, was determined that his daughter Tannoch would marry a prince called Ewan, but the young girl, who had become a Christian, preferred to dedicate herself to the service of God. She was cast out but found shelter with a swineherd and his companions, where she quickly settled into a new and peaceful life. However, this was soon disturbed by Ewan; finding her alone one day, he violated Tannoch and she became pregnant.

Discovering the shame of his unmarried daughter, Loth resolved to have her thrown down the sheer 700-foot drop called Dunpelder on the south side of Traprain Law. As she fell, Tannoch was heard to call upon the Blessed Virgin Mary for aid.

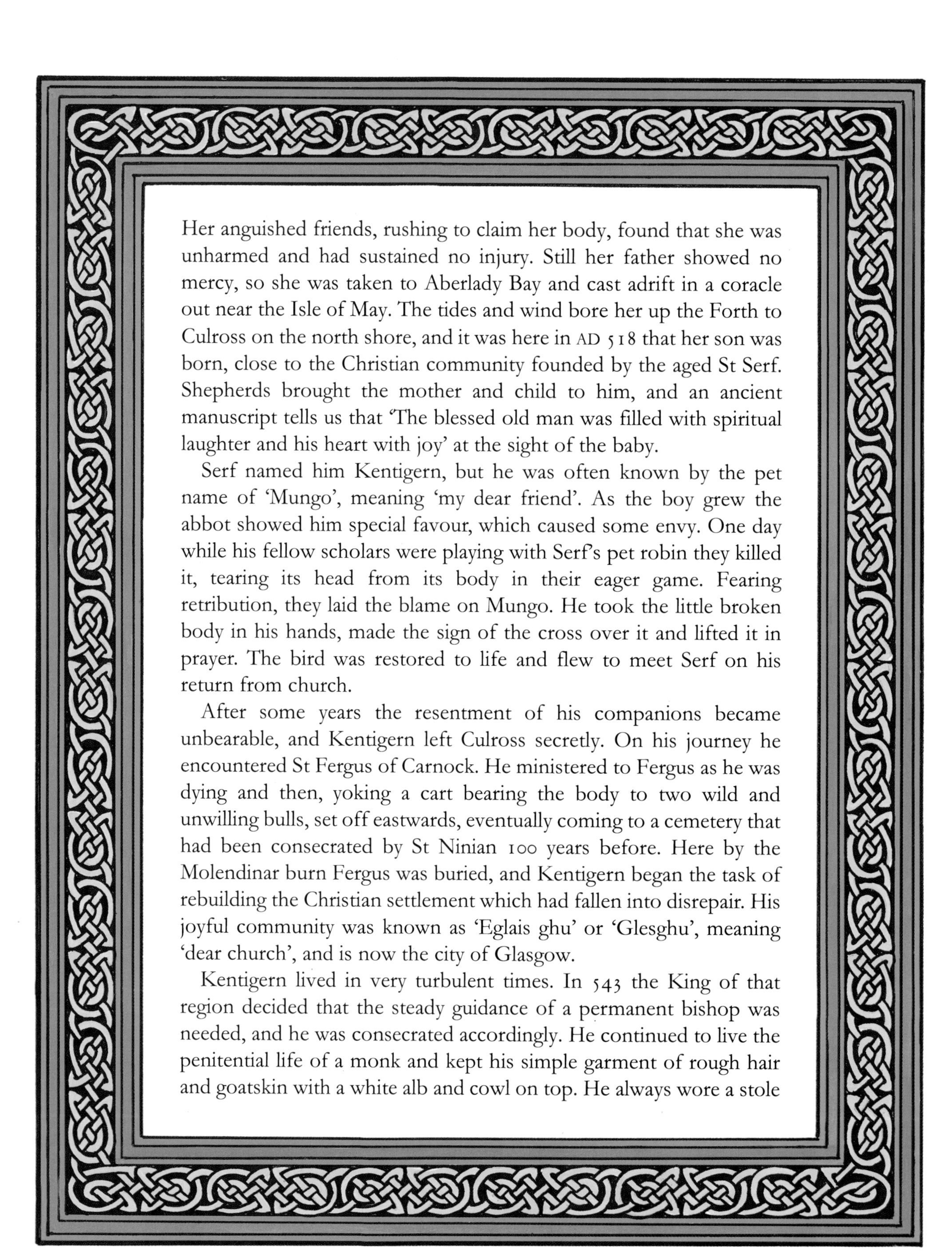

Her anguished friends, rushing to claim her body, found that she was unharmed and had sustained no injury. Still her father showed no mercy, so she was taken to Aberlady Bay and cast adrift in a coracle out near the Isle of May. The tides and wind bore her up the Forth to Culross on the north shore, and it was here in AD 518 that her son was born, close to the Christian community founded by the aged St Serf. Shepherds brought the mother and child to him, and an ancient manuscript tells us that 'The blessed old man was filled with spiritual laughter and his heart with joy' at the sight of the baby.

Serf named him Kentigern, but he was often known by the pet name of 'Mungo', meaning 'my dear friend'. As the boy grew the abbot showed him special favour, which caused some envy. One day while his fellow scholars were playing with Serf's pet robin they killed it, tearing its head from its body in their eager game. Fearing retribution, they laid the blame on Mungo. He took the little broken body in his hands, made the sign of the cross over it and lifted it in prayer. The bird was restored to life and flew to meet Serf on his return from church.

After some years the resentment of his companions became unbearable, and Kentigern left Culross secretly. On his journey he encountered St Fergus of Carnock. He ministered to Fergus as he was dying and then, yoking a cart bearing the body to two wild and unwilling bulls, set off eastwards, eventually coming to a cemetery that had been consecrated by St Ninian 100 years before. Here by the Molendinar burn Fergus was buried, and Kentigern began the task of rebuilding the Christian settlement which had fallen into disrepair. His joyful community was known as 'Eglais ghu' or 'Glesghu', meaning 'dear church', and is now the city of Glasgow.

Kentigern lived in very turbulent times. In 543 the King of that region decided that the steady guidance of a permanent bishop was needed, and he was consecrated accordingly. He continued to live the penitential life of a monk and kept his simple garment of rough hair and goatskin with a white alb and cowl on top. He always wore a stole

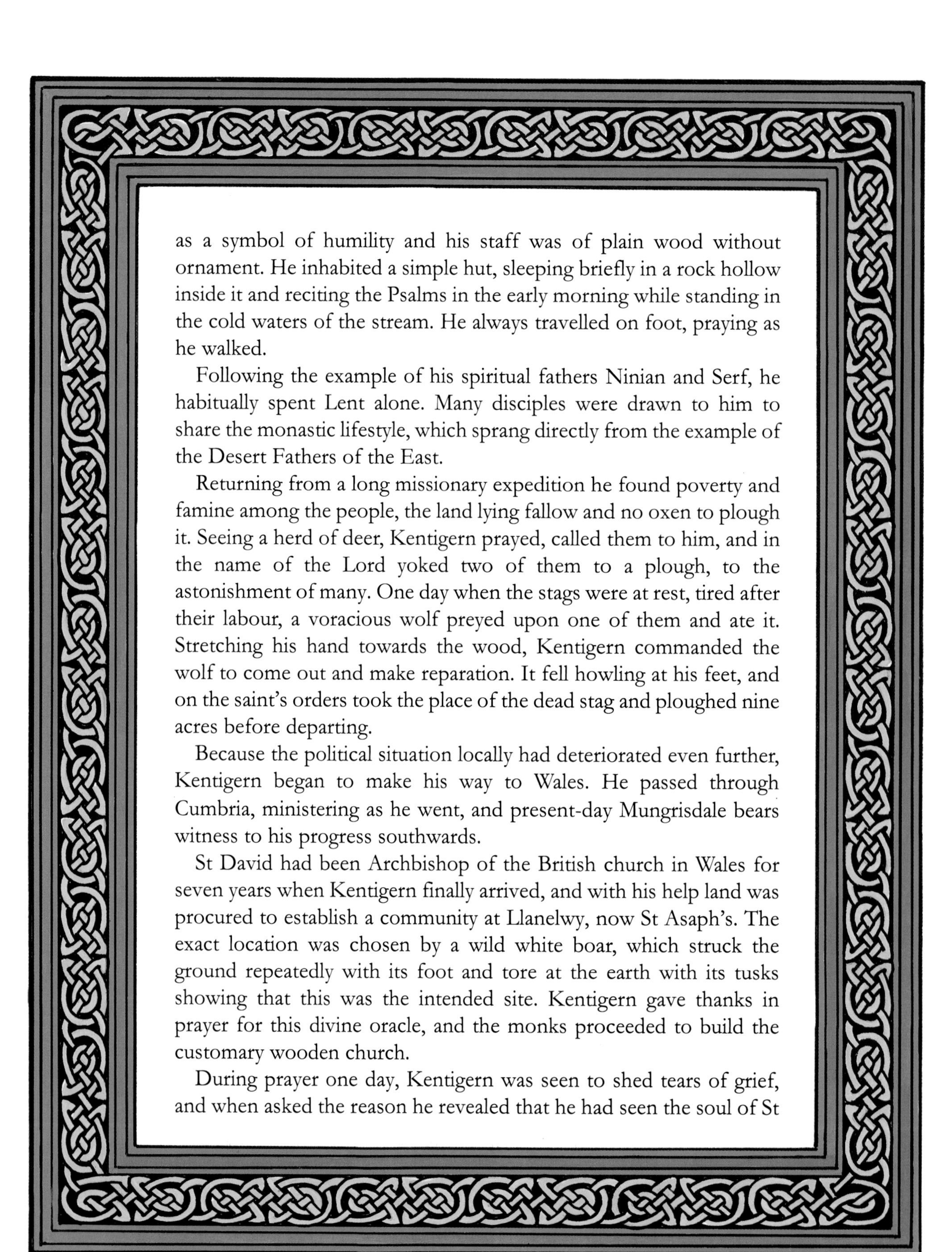

as a symbol of humility and his staff was of plain wood without ornament. He inhabited a simple hut, sleeping briefly in a rock hollow inside it and reciting the Psalms in the early morning while standing in the cold waters of the stream. He always travelled on foot, praying as he walked.

Following the example of his spiritual fathers Ninian and Serf, he habitually spent Lent alone. Many disciples were drawn to him to share the monastic lifestyle, which sprang directly from the example of the Desert Fathers of the East.

Returning from a long missionary expedition he found poverty and famine among the people, the land lying fallow and no oxen to plough it. Seeing a herd of deer, Kentigern prayed, called them to him, and in the name of the Lord yoked two of them to a plough, to the astonishment of many. One day when the stags were at rest, tired after their labour, a voracious wolf preyed upon one of them and ate it. Stretching his hand towards the wood, Kentigern commanded the wolf to come out and make reparation. It fell howling at his feet, and on the saint's orders took the place of the dead stag and ploughed nine acres before departing.

Because the political situation locally had deteriorated even further, Kentigern began to make his way to Wales. He passed through Cumbria, ministering as he went, and present-day Mungrisdale bears witness to his progress southwards.

St David had been Archbishop of the British church in Wales for seven years when Kentigern finally arrived, and with his help land was procured to establish a community at Llanelwy, now St Asaph's. The exact location was chosen by a wild white boar, which struck the ground repeatedly with its foot and tore at the earth with its tusks showing that this was the intended site. Kentigern gave thanks in prayer for this divine oracle, and the monks proceeded to build the customary wooden church.

During prayer one day, Kentigern was seen to shed tears of grief, and when asked the reason he revealed that he had seen the soul of St

David ascending to heaven. Later when they sent to Menevia for news the death was confirmed.

After some time King Rederech sent messengers to Wales requesting Kentigern to return. He hesitated, but heard an angel voice saying, 'Go back to Glasgow thy church . . .' Kentigern enthroned Asaph as his successor and set out, but instead of returning to Glasgow straightaway he made his base at Hoddam in Dumfries and Galloway and stayed there for some years. Eventually he was reinstated in Glasgow nearly thirty years after his departure. He was responsible for an extensive mission to Aberdeenshire, and there is evidence that his disciples travelled as far afield as Orkney, Norway and Iceland. Kentigern himself visited Pope Gregory in Rome and received among other treasures the gift of a bell, which was later used in the streets of the city as a summons to prayer for the dead.

Probably the best-known story of the saint is that concerning Laguoreth, the wife of King

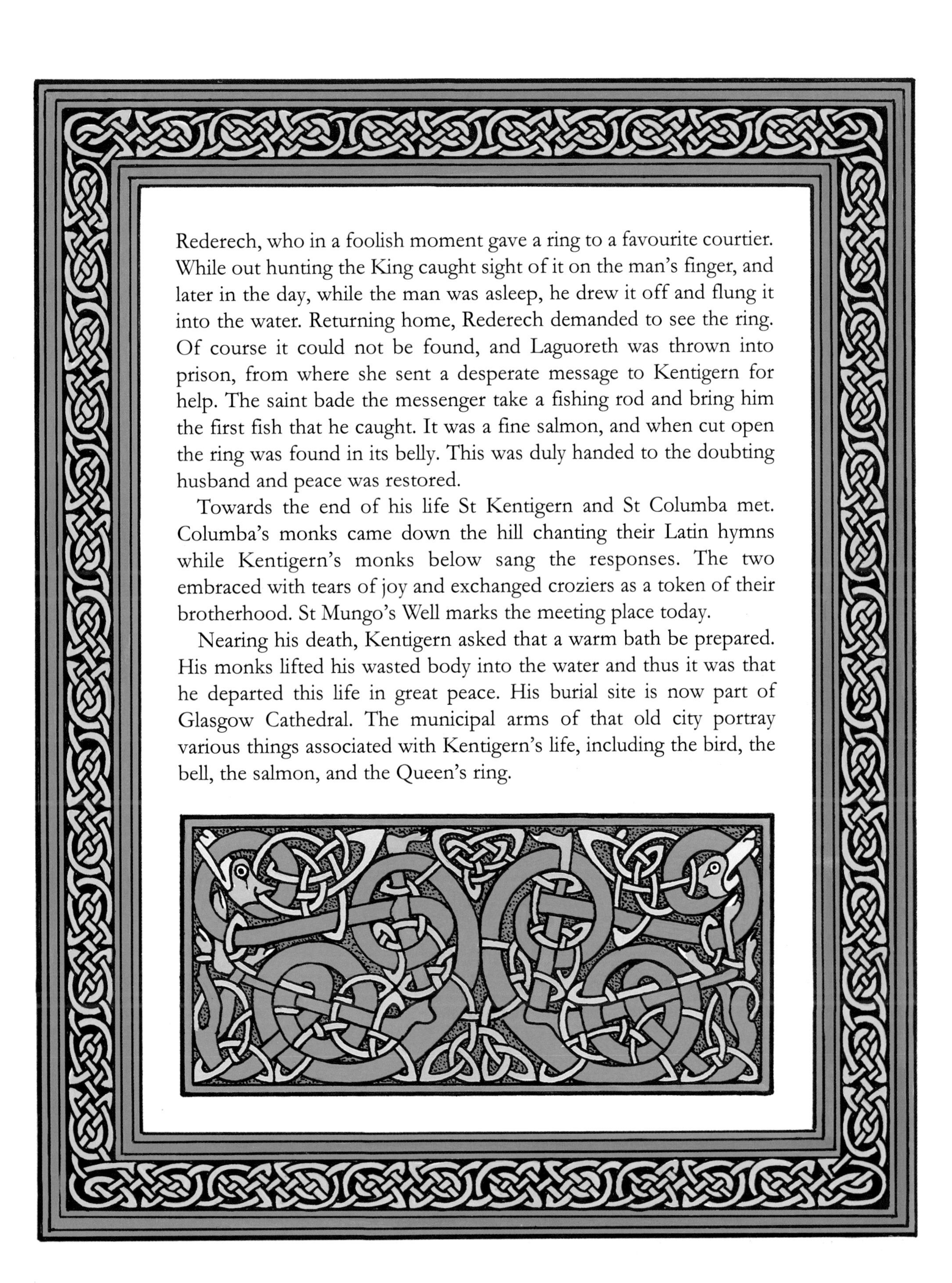

Rederech, who in a foolish moment gave a ring to a favourite courtier. While out hunting the King caught sight of it on the man's finger, and later in the day, while the man was asleep, he drew it off and flung it into the water. Returning home, Rederech demanded to see the ring. Of course it could not be found, and Laguoreth was thrown into prison, from where she sent a desperate message to Kentigern for help. The saint bade the messenger take a fishing rod and bring him the first fish that he caught. It was a fine salmon, and when cut open the ring was found in its belly. This was duly handed to the doubting husband and peace was restored.

Towards the end of his life St Kentigern and St Columba met. Columba's monks came down the hill chanting their Latin hymns while Kentigern's monks below sang the responses. The two embraced with tears of joy and exchanged croziers as a token of their brotherhood. St Mungo's Well marks the meeting place today.

Nearing his death, Kentigern asked that a warm bath be prepared. His monks lifted his wasted body into the water and thus it was that he departed this life in great peace. His burial site is now part of Glasgow Cathedral. The municipal arms of that old city portray various things associated with Kentigern's life, including the bird, the bell, the salmon, and the Queen's ring.

Petroc

FEAST DAY: 4 June

Now dwelleth Petroc with the Saints in glory,
But, ever mindful of the soil he planted,
Though parted from us, poureth supplications,
Pleading for Cornwall.

Extract from *St Petroc's Hymn* by Athelstan Riley

St Petroc has the distinction of being the most influential of the Cornish saints and rivals St Piran for the privilege of being patron of that nation. St Michael the Archangel, who has been adopted by all the Celtic countries, is also a contender.

Petroc came from South Wales, from the royal house of Gwent, and was the uncle of St Cadoc. Quite often the saints are interrelated in this way, showing how entire households accepted the light of the gospel. He embarked upon the monastic life at a very early age and after some years travelled to Ireland to further his studies, remaining there for twenty years or so before settling beside the Camel estuary in Cornwall at Petrocstow, which has become

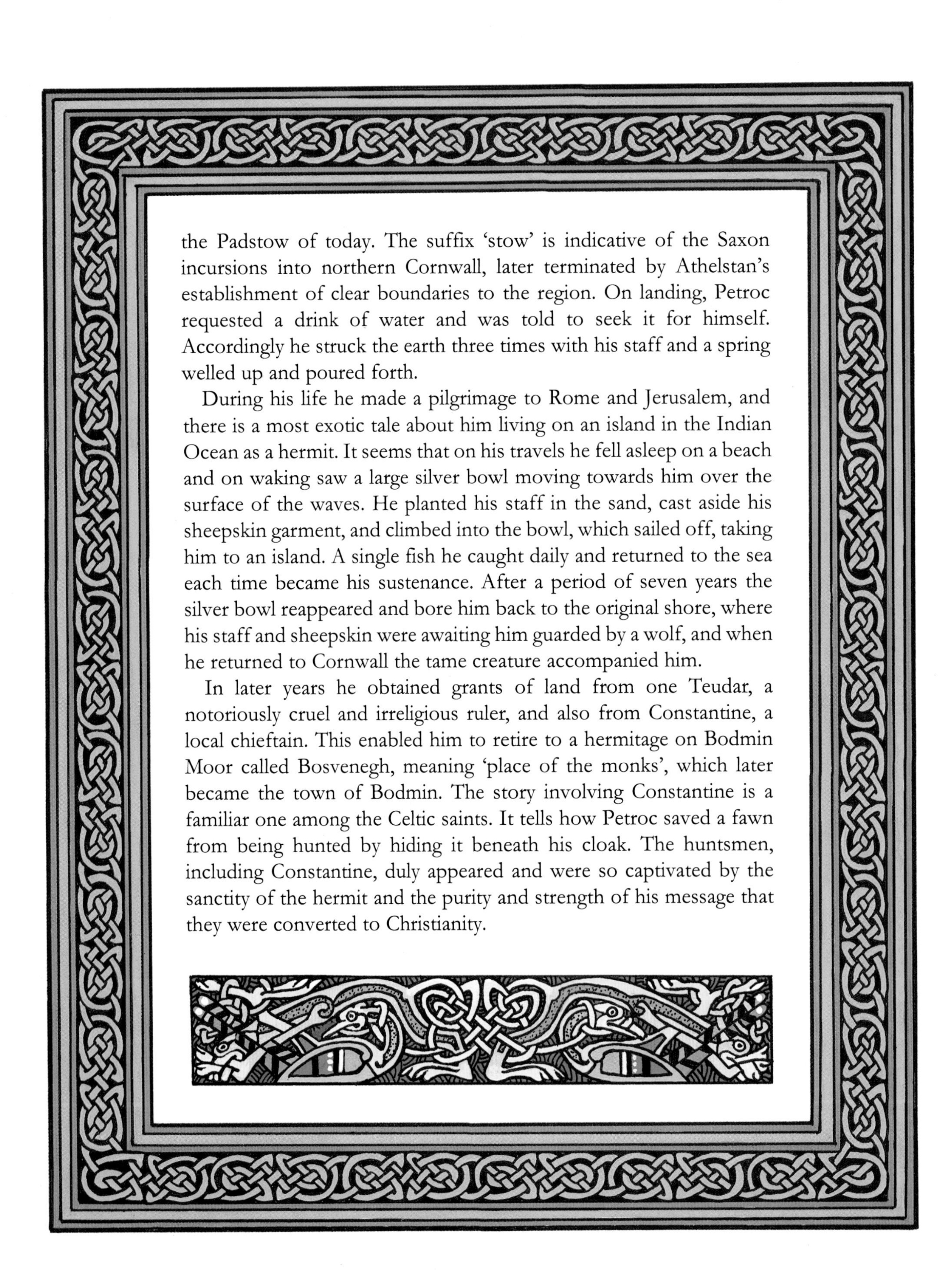

the Padstow of today. The suffix 'stow' is indicative of the Saxon incursions into northern Cornwall, later terminated by Athelstan's establishment of clear boundaries to the region. On landing, Petroc requested a drink of water and was told to seek it for himself. Accordingly he struck the earth three times with his staff and a spring welled up and poured forth.

During his life he made a pilgrimage to Rome and Jerusalem, and there is a most exotic tale about him living on an island in the Indian Ocean as a hermit. It seems that on his travels he fell asleep on a beach and on waking saw a large silver bowl moving towards him over the surface of the waves. He planted his staff in the sand, cast aside his sheepskin garment, and climbed into the bowl, which sailed off, taking him to an island. A single fish he caught daily and returned to the sea each time became his sustenance. After a period of seven years the silver bowl reappeared and bore him back to the original shore, where his staff and sheepskin were awaiting him guarded by a wolf, and when he returned to Cornwall the tame creature accompanied him.

In later years he obtained grants of land from one Teudar, a notoriously cruel and irreligious ruler, and also from Constantine, a local chieftain. This enabled him to retire to a hermitage on Bodmin Moor called Bosvenegh, meaning 'place of the monks', which later became the town of Bodmin. The story involving Constantine is a familiar one among the Celtic saints. It tells how Petroc saved a fawn from being hunted by hiding it beneath his cloak. The huntsmen, including Constantine, duly appeared and were so captivated by the sanctity of the hermit and the purity and strength of his message that they were converted to Christianity.

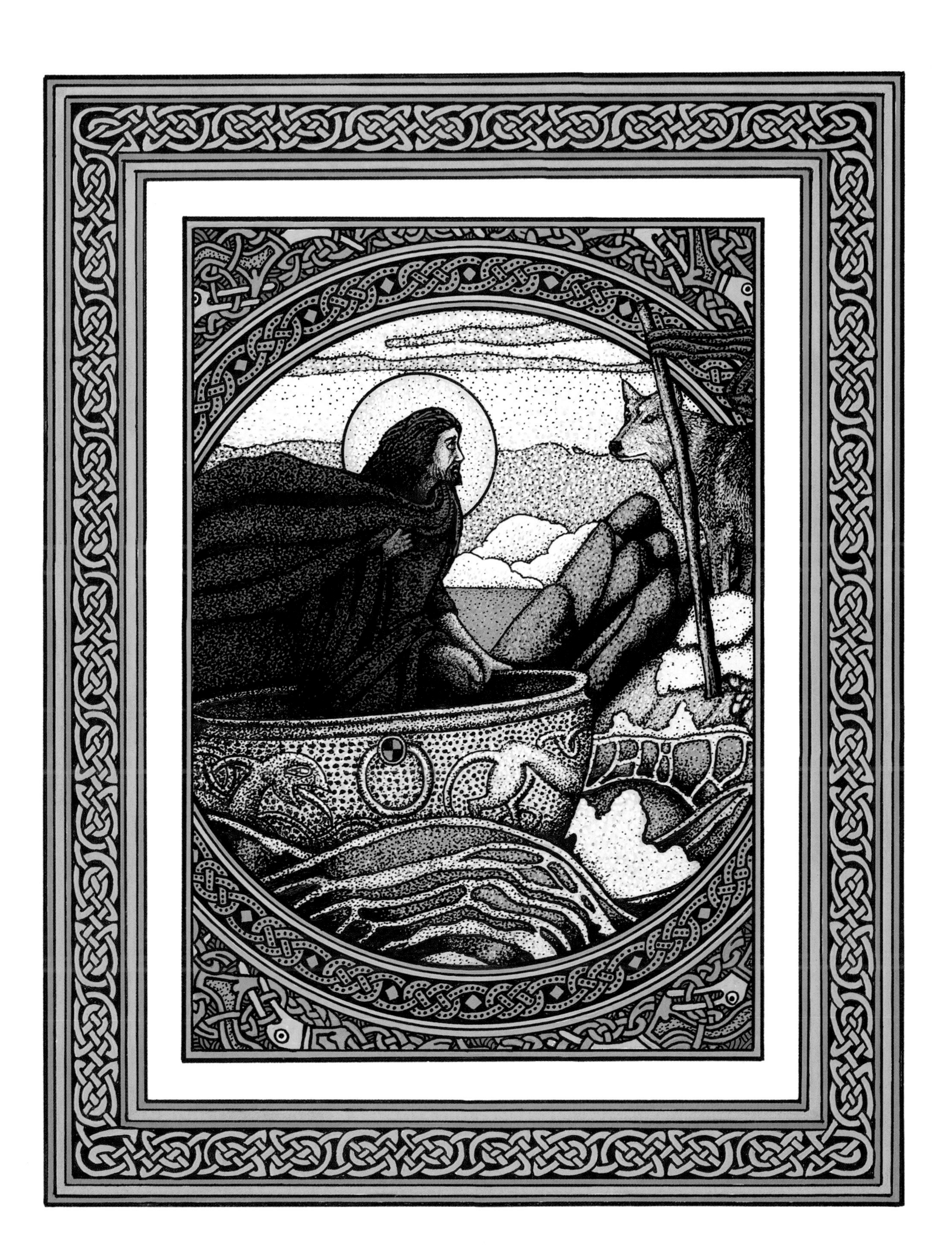

When Petroc sensed that death was near he set out on a journey to bid farewell to his communities. While resting near to Little Petherick (also known as Petroc Minor), he entered the home of a man named Rovel and his family and there he died in June 564. There is still a farm in this vicinity called Treravel. He was buried at Padstow but later his body was removed to Bodmin, which by the eleventh century had become a centre of veneration for St Petroc. In 1177 his relics were stolen by a Breton priest and taken to St Méen in Brittany. The intervention of Henry II, who was overlord of Brittany, was sought, and the King was instrumental in the return of the relics to Bodmin Priory.

In 1957 the ivory casket, rich in Arab craftsmanship, which had once contained St Petroc's bones was returned to Bodmin parish church but his staff, and his bell which was lost shortly before the reign of Henry I, have never been found.

Petroc is sometimes depicted with a dragon and has at least two

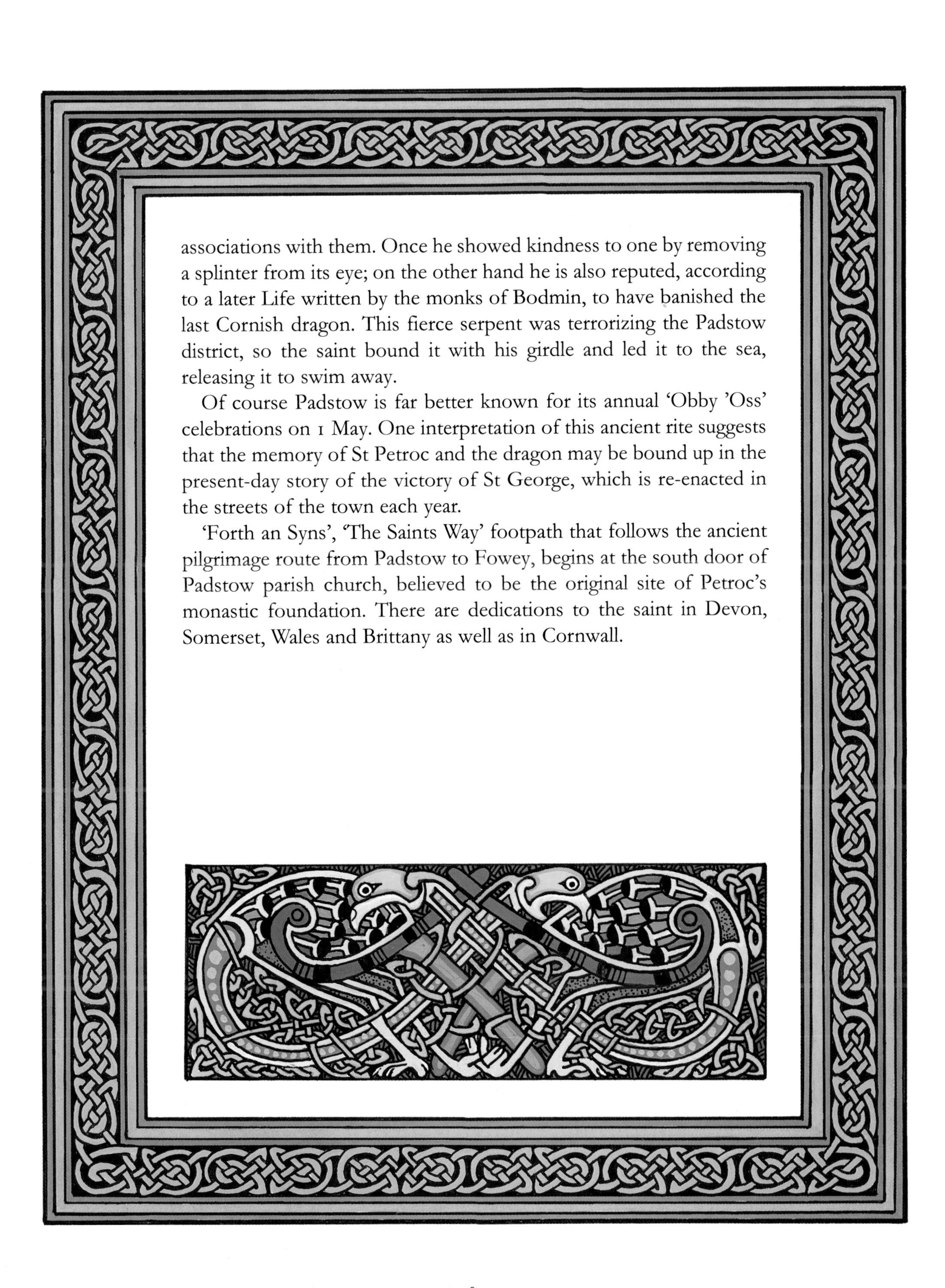

associations with them. Once he showed kindness to one by removing a splinter from its eye; on the other hand he is also reputed, according to a later Life written by the monks of Bodmin, to have banished the last Cornish dragon. This fierce serpent was terrorizing the Padstow district, so the saint bound it with his girdle and led it to the sea, releasing it to swim away.

Of course Padstow is far better known for its annual 'Obby 'Oss' celebrations on 1 May. One interpretation of this ancient rite suggests that the memory of St Petroc and the dragon may be bound up in the present-day story of the victory of St George, which is re-enacted in the streets of the town each year.

'Forth an Syns', 'The Saints Way' footpath that follows the ancient pilgrimage route from Padstow to Fowey, begins at the south door of Padstow parish church, believed to be the original site of Petroc's monastic foundation. There are dedications to the saint in Devon, Somerset, Wales and Brittany as well as in Cornwall.

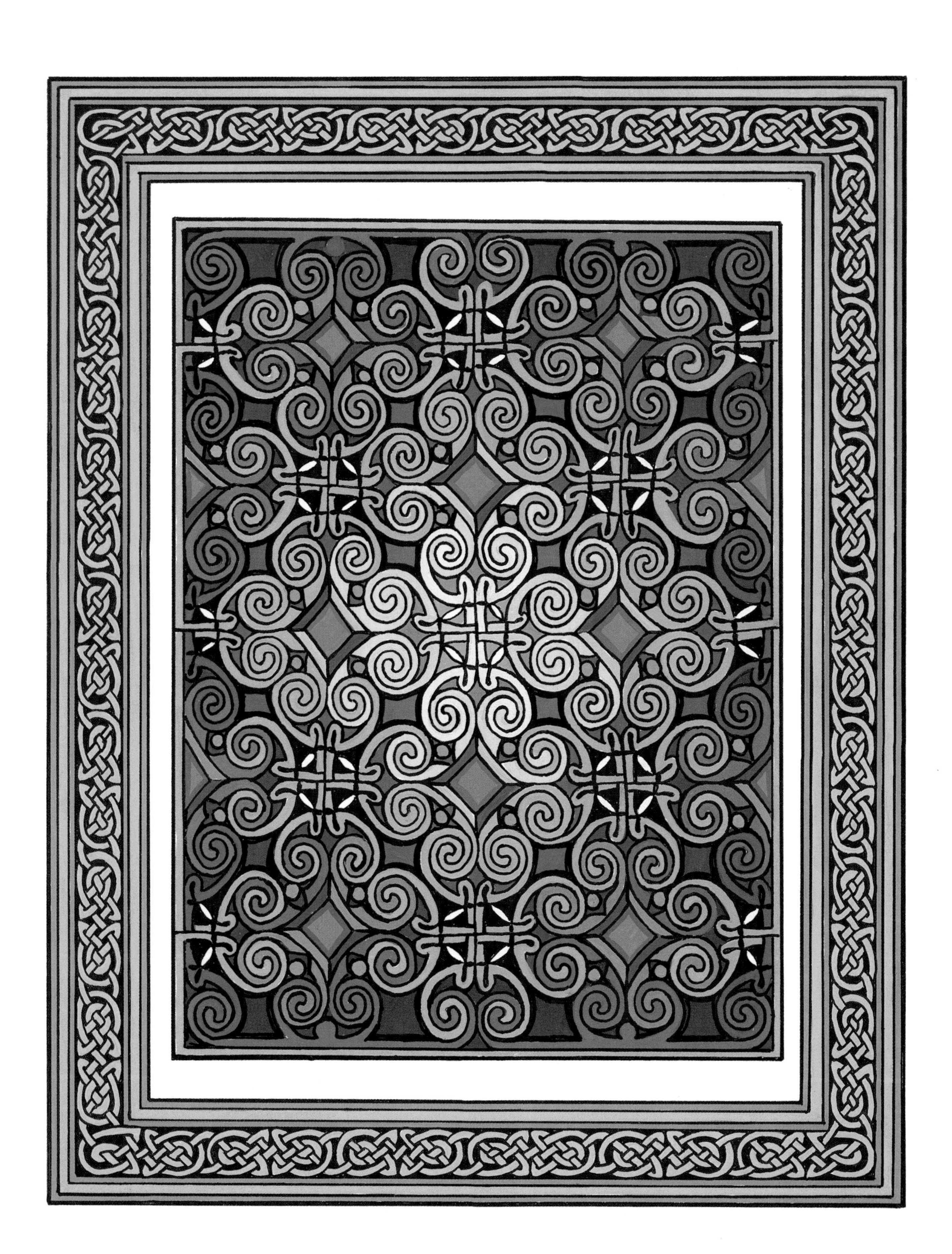

Piran

FEAST DAY: 5 March

The Lord has revealed in the fullness of time, and at the very moment I needed it, where the mystic metal lies, beneath stony useless ground: and I leave it to you good people, and you holy saints, to interpret what it means. But sure to God, 'tis a sign enough for meself, and nothing now will deprive me of my bishopric and the true care of my flock!

From *The Trials of St Piran*, a play by Donald Rawe

One stormy day a band of wild pagan Irishmen decided to rid themselves of St Piran because, in spite of his great goodness, they were afraid of his authority and power and envious of his influence on the people of their territories. They chained him to a millstone, took him to the cliff-top, and cast him into the raging sea below, supposedly to his death. As he fell, the ferocious winds dropped to a gentle whisper, the sea became as smooth as glass and the sun broke through the clouds to reveal the saint sitting on the stone, which floated away, bearing him to the Cornish shore. He landed at Perranporth on 5 March, which has become his feast day. It is thought that this legend concerning the millstone

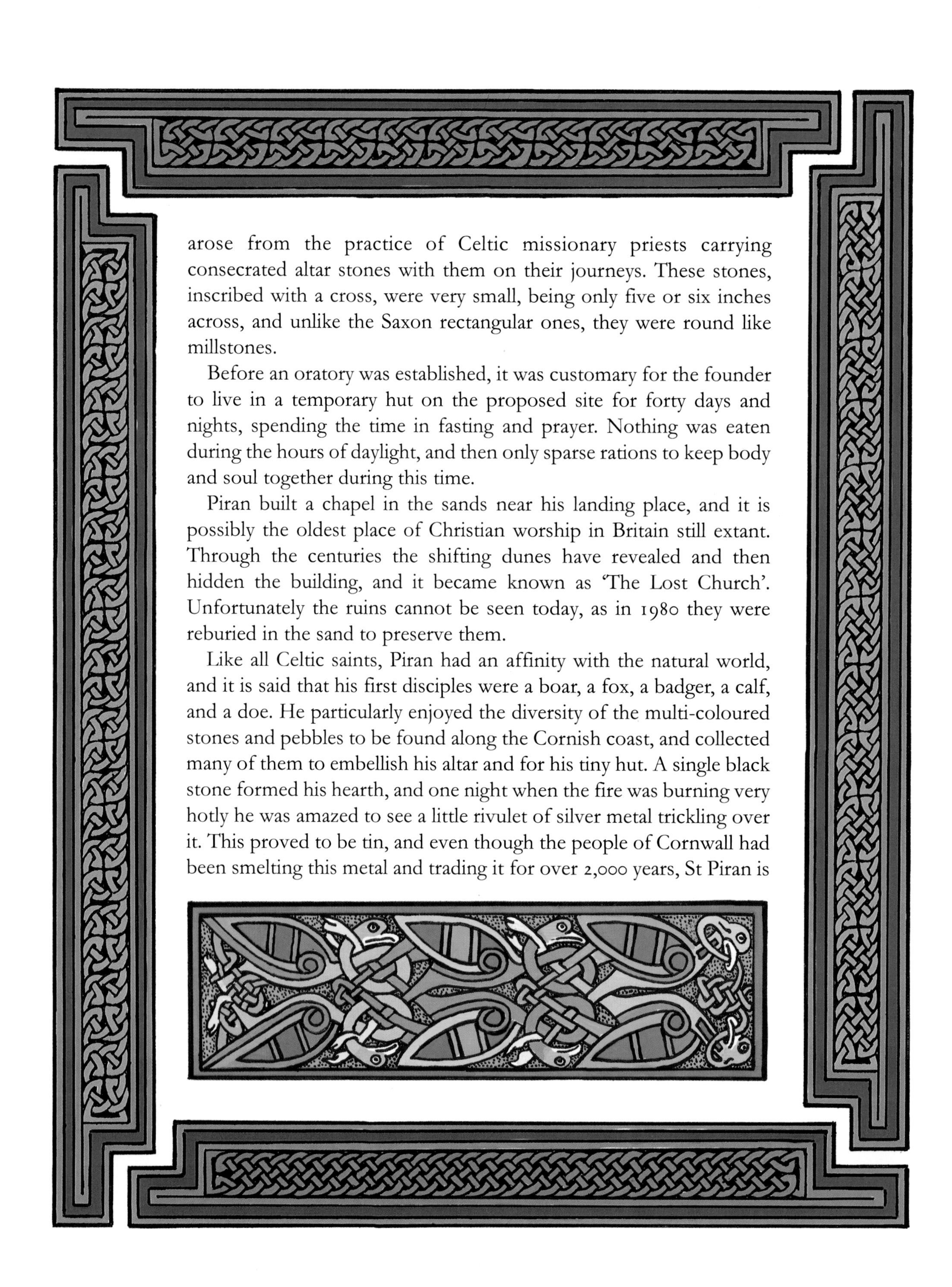

arose from the practice of Celtic missionary priests carrying consecrated altar stones with them on their journeys. These stones, inscribed with a cross, were very small, being only five or six inches across, and unlike the Saxon rectangular ones, they were round like millstones.

Before an oratory was established, it was customary for the founder to live in a temporary hut on the proposed site for forty days and nights, spending the time in fasting and prayer. Nothing was eaten during the hours of daylight, and then only sparse rations to keep body and soul together during this time.

Piran built a chapel in the sands near his landing place, and it is possibly the oldest place of Christian worship in Britain still extant. Through the centuries the shifting dunes have revealed and then hidden the building, and it became known as 'The Lost Church'. Unfortunately the ruins cannot be seen today, as in 1980 they were reburied in the sand to preserve them.

Like all Celtic saints, Piran had an affinity with the natural world, and it is said that his first disciples were a boar, a fox, a badger, a calf, and a doe. He particularly enjoyed the diversity of the multi-coloured stones and pebbles to be found along the Cornish coast, and collected many of them to embellish his altar and for his tiny hut. A single black stone formed his hearth, and one night when the fire was burning very hotly he was amazed to see a little rivulet of silver metal trickling over it. This proved to be tin, and even though the people of Cornwall had been smelting this metal and trading it for over 2,000 years, St Piran is

credited with discovering this process and was adopted by the miners as their patron saint. The Cornish national flag is known as 'St Piran's Cross' and consists of a white cross on a black ground, said to represent the metal in the ore as well as the light of the Christian faith in the darkness of the world.

This sixth-century abbot is honoured not only in Cornwall but in South Wales and Brittany too. Gerald of Wales tells us that there was a chapel in Cardiff dedicated to St Piran. It was here that King Henry II celebrated Mass when he returned from Ireland. As he was leaving, a tall, fair man clad in a white robe admonished him, telling him to mend his ways and to prohibit trading on Sundays or misfortune would befall him. The King left the chapel, but before he reached the gate he sent one of his attendants to search for the stranger who could not be found. Henry disregarded the advice and within the year the prediction proved true. In Brittany, between St Pol-de-Léon and

Lesneven, there is a flat stone beside the road known as 'St Piran's Bed'. The hollows in it are said to have been made by the knees of the saint in prayer.

Tradition tells that he died at the age of 206 and was buried with his mother in his chapel. Certainly his head was kept in a reliquary and a processional bier held his body. His pastoral staff, covered with gold and silver and set with precious stones, a silver cross containing small relics of the saint, and a copper bell were also preserved. Sadly all these treasures have now been lost.

In the Middle Ages 'St Piran's Feast' was kept as a holiday in Cornwall, and there are three parishes in the county that still recall his name: Perran-ar-Worthal, Perranzabuloe, and Perranuthnoe.

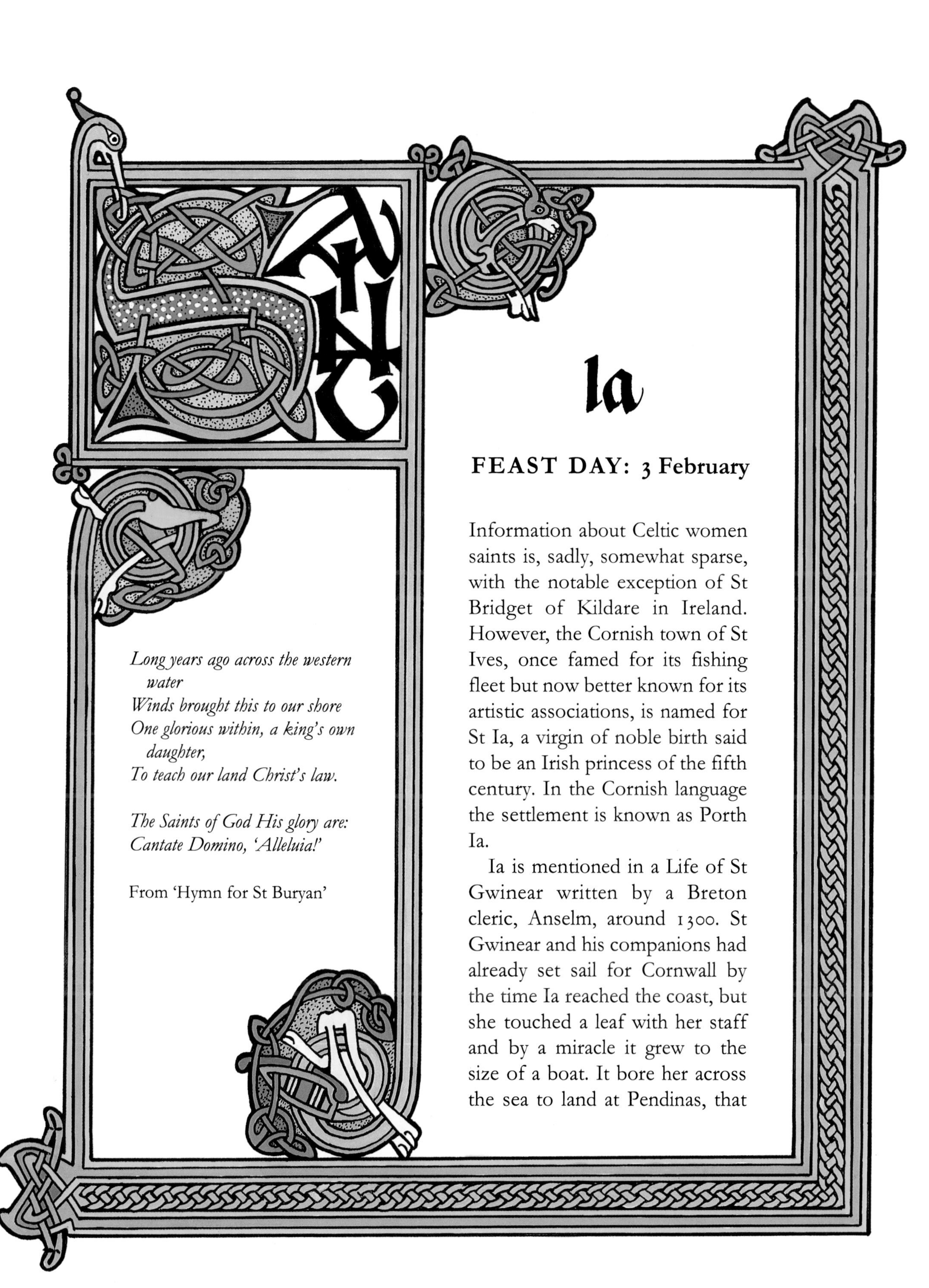

Ia

FEAST DAY: 3 February

Long years ago across the western
water
Winds brought this to our shore
One glorious within, a king's own
daughter,
To teach our land Christ's law.

The Saints of God His glory are:
Cantate Domino, 'Alleluia!'

From 'Hymn for St Buryan'

Information about Celtic women saints is, sadly, somewhat sparse, with the notable exception of St Bridget of Kildare in Ireland. However, the Cornish town of St Ives, once famed for its fishing fleet but now better known for its artistic associations, is named for St Ia, a virgin of noble birth said to be an Irish princess of the fifth century. In the Cornish language the settlement is known as Porth Ia.

Ia is mentioned in a Life of St Gwinear written by a Breton cleric, Anselm, around 1300. St Gwinear and his companions had already set sail for Cornwall by the time Ia reached the coast, but she touched a leaf with her staff and by a miracle it grew to the size of a boat. It bore her across the sea to land at Pendinas, that

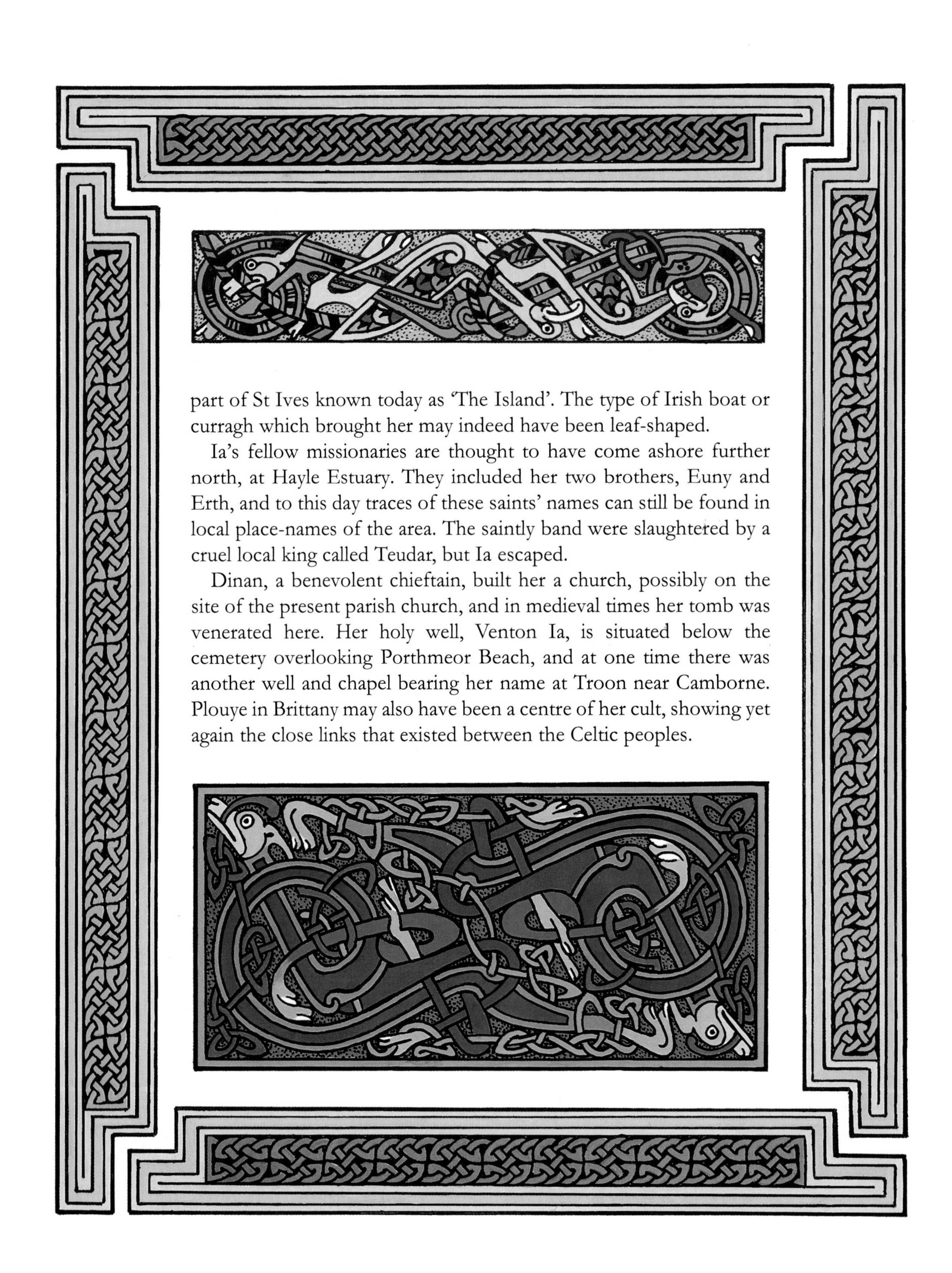

part of St Ives known today as 'The Island'. The type of Irish boat or curragh which brought her may indeed have been leaf-shaped.

Ia's fellow missionaries are thought to have come ashore further north, at Hayle Estuary. They included her two brothers, Euny and Erth, and to this day traces of these saints' names can still be found in local place-names of the area. The saintly band were slaughtered by a cruel local king called Teudar, but Ia escaped.

Dinan, a benevolent chieftain, built her a church, possibly on the site of the present parish church, and in medieval times her tomb was venerated here. Her holy well, Venton Ia, is situated below the cemetery overlooking Porthmeor Beach, and at one time there was another well and chapel bearing her name at Troon near Camborne. Plouye in Brittany may also have been a centre of her cult, showing yet again the close links that existed between the Celtic peoples.

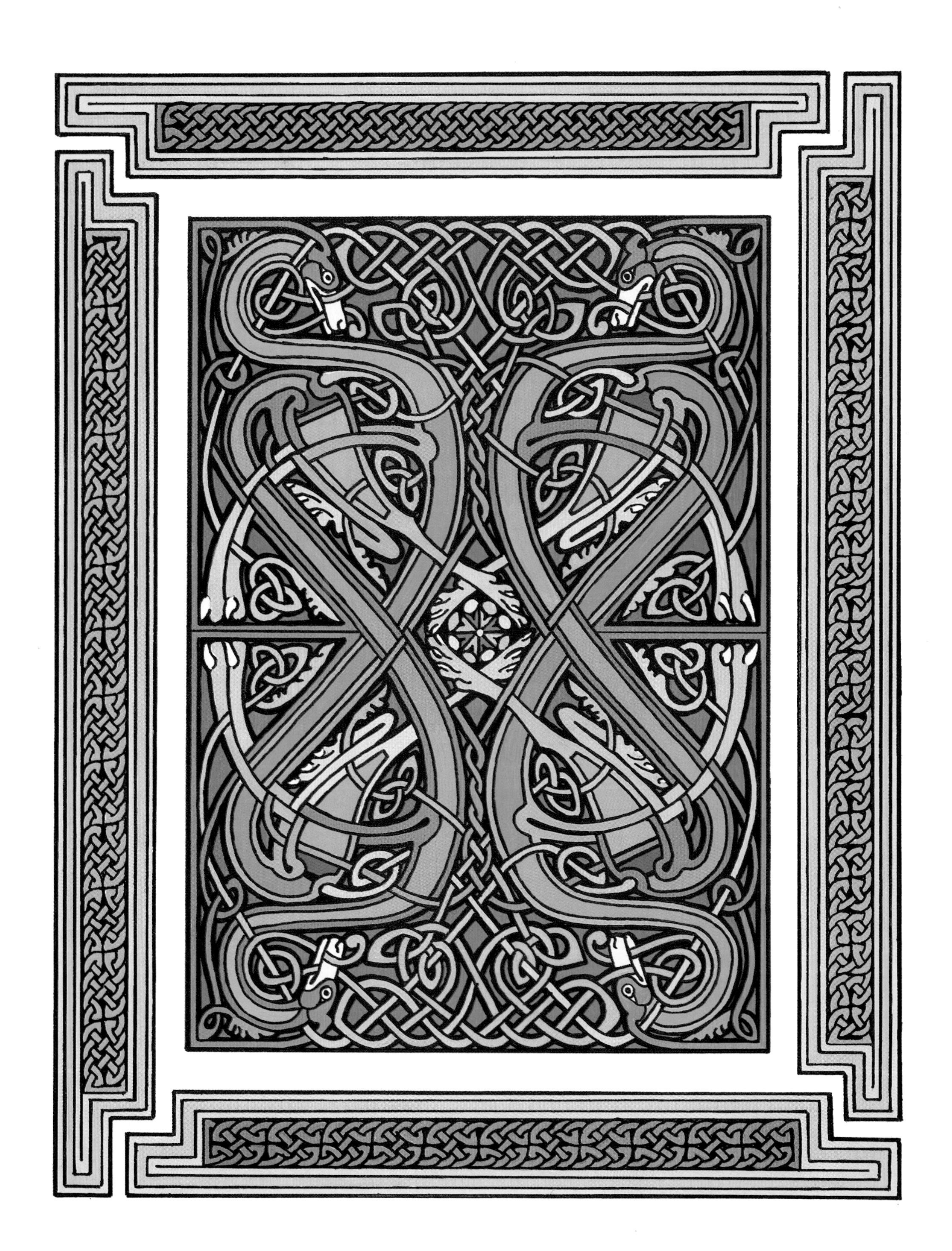

Kevin

FEAST DAY: 3 June

Coemghen is the Irish form of the name of the saint we have come to know as Kevin. The name means 'of gentle birth', for because her offspring was innocent, faithful and righteous, his mother Caemell or Coenhella experienced no labour pains. Born of royal lineage in Leinster in the sixth century, he came from a family of saints. Twelve angels with golden lamps presided at his birth.

He was taken to a priest for baptism and given the name Kevin as the angels had commanded. Cronan, the priest, prophesied that kings and chieftains would come to the faith through him.

Kevin spent his early childhood years at the Fort of the White Fountain. While he dwelt

A glen without threshing floor or
corn rick,
Only rugged rock above it,
A glen where no one is refused
refreshment,
The Grace of the Lord is there.

From a tenth-century life
of St Kevin

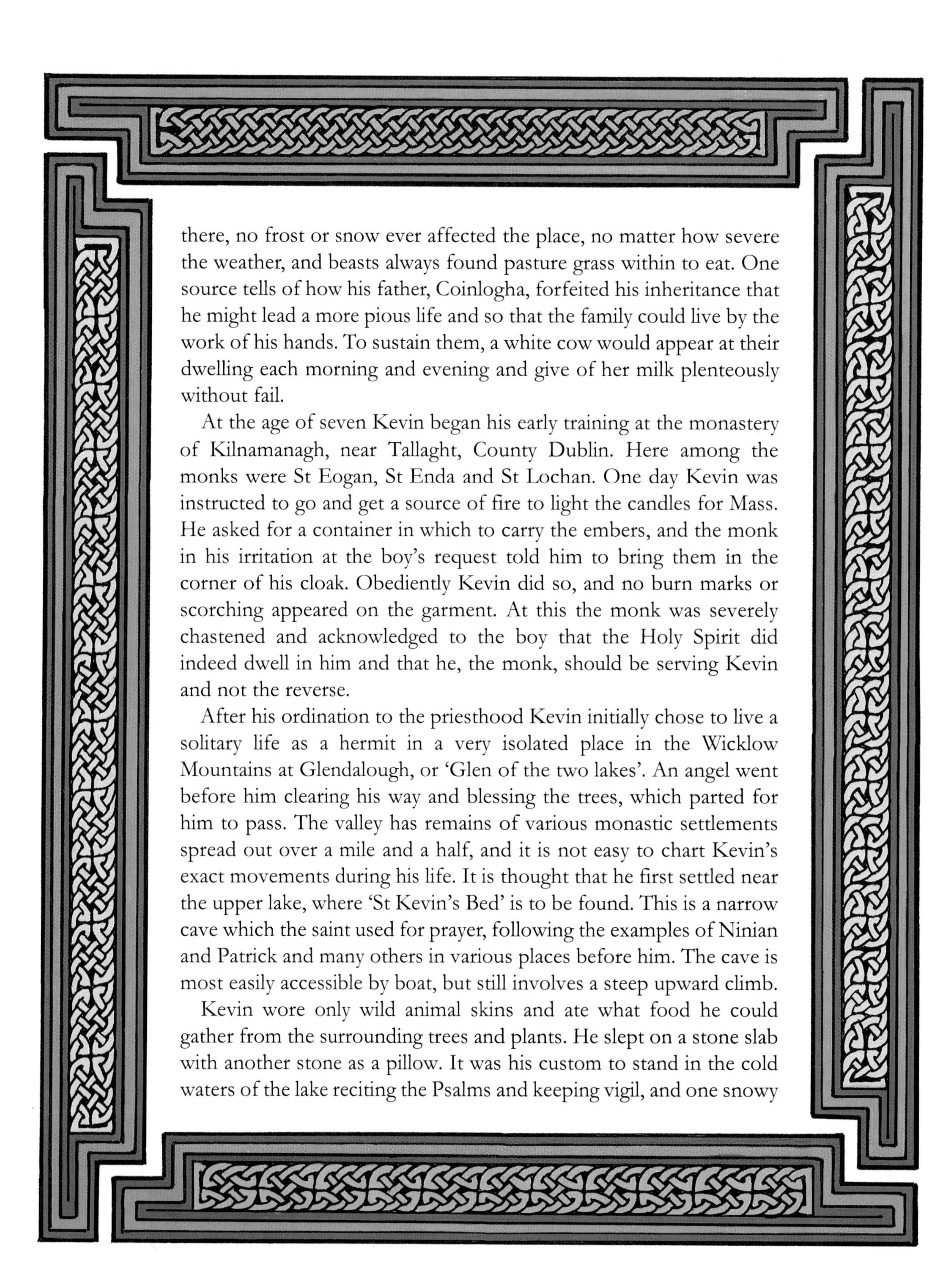

there, no frost or snow ever affected the place, no matter how severe the weather, and beasts always found pasture grass within to eat. One source tells of how his father, Coinlogha, forfeited his inheritance that he might lead a more pious life and so that the family could live by the work of his hands. To sustain them, a white cow would appear at their dwelling each morning and evening and give of her milk plenteously without fail.

At the age of seven Kevin began his early training at the monastery of Kilnamanagh, near Tallaght, County Dublin. Here among the monks were St Eogan, St Enda and St Lochan. One day Kevin was instructed to go and get a source of fire to light the candles for Mass. He asked for a container in which to carry the embers, and the monk in his irritation at the boy's request told him to bring them in the corner of his cloak. Obediently Kevin did so, and no burn marks or scorching appeared on the garment. At this the monk was severely chastened and acknowledged to the boy that the Holy Spirit did indeed dwell in him and that he, the monk, should be serving Kevin and not the reverse.

After his ordination to the priesthood Kevin initially chose to live a solitary life as a hermit in a very isolated place in the Wicklow Mountains at Glendalough, or 'Glen of the two lakes'. An angel went before him clearing his way and blessing the trees, which parted for him to pass. The valley has remains of various monastic settlements spread out over a mile and a half, and it is not easy to chart Kevin's exact movements during his life. It is thought that he first settled near the upper lake, where 'St Kevin's Bed' is to be found. This is a narrow cave which the saint used for prayer, following the examples of Ninian and Patrick and many others in various places before him. The cave is most easily accessible by boat, but still involves a steep upward climb.

Kevin wore only wild animal skins and ate what food he could gather from the surrounding trees and plants. He slept on a stone slab with another stone as a pillow. It was his custom to stand in the cold waters of the lake reciting the Psalms and keeping vigil, and one snowy

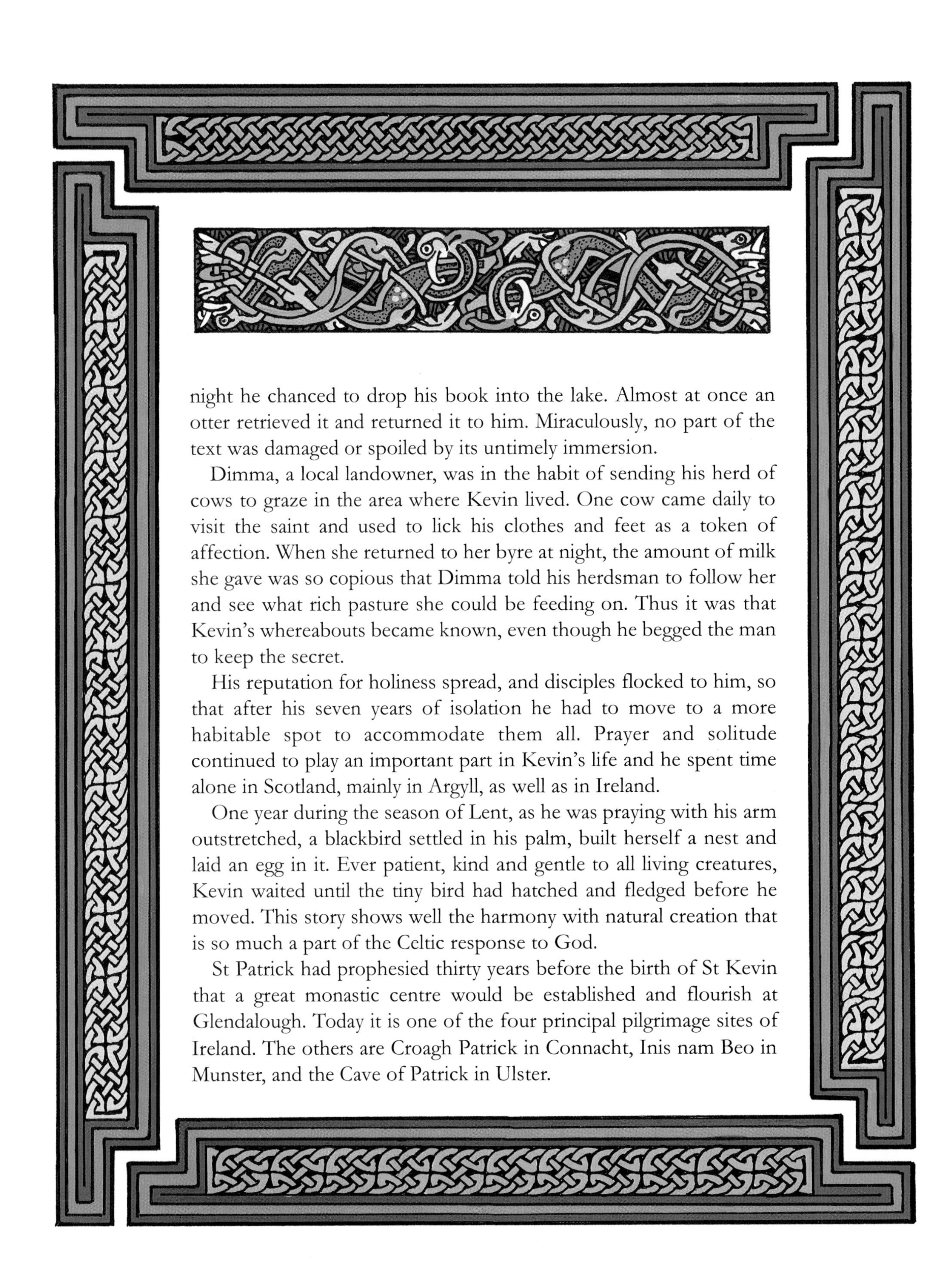

night he chanced to drop his book into the lake. Almost at once an otter retrieved it and returned it to him. Miraculously, no part of the text was damaged or spoiled by its untimely immersion.

Dimma, a local landowner, was in the habit of sending his herd of cows to graze in the area where Kevin lived. One cow came daily to visit the saint and used to lick his clothes and feet as a token of affection. When she returned to her byre at night, the amount of milk she gave was so copious that Dimma told his herdsman to follow her and see what rich pasture she could be feeding on. Thus it was that Kevin's whereabouts became known, even though he begged the man to keep the secret.

His reputation for holiness spread, and disciples flocked to him, so that after his seven years of isolation he had to move to a more habitable spot to accommodate them all. Prayer and solitude continued to play an important part in Kevin's life and he spent time alone in Scotland, mainly in Argyll, as well as in Ireland.

One year during the season of Lent, as he was praying with his arm outstretched, a blackbird settled in his palm, built herself a nest and laid an egg in it. Ever patient, kind and gentle to all living creatures, Kevin waited until the tiny bird had hatched and fledged before he moved. This story shows well the harmony with natural creation that is so much a part of the Celtic response to God.

St Patrick had prophesied thirty years before the birth of St Kevin that a great monastic centre would be established and flourish at Glendalough. Today it is one of the four principal pilgrimage sites of Ireland. The others are Croagh Patrick in Connacht, Inis nam Beo in Munster, and the Cave of Patrick in Ulster.

Poetry and music were among St Kevin's gifts, and his harp was one of the greatest treasures of Glendalough as late as the twelfth century. The rule for his monks was written in verse. Many young boys came there to be trained in the religious life, and there is a legend that tells how a boy in Kevin's care asked for an apple out of season. The saint blessed a nearby tree, which immediately bore fruit. The historian Gerald of Wales mentions a willow-like tree on the site which bore apples each year. These were known as 'St Kevin's apples' and were in great demand throughout the whole of Ireland.

Until 1835 there was, near the portals of the cathedral, a yew tree reputed to have been planted by Kevin. Sadly, it was cut down to make furniture, and many people came to gather up the fragments as mementoes of the saint.

It is thought that Kevin was over 120 years old when he died in about AD 618. Before his death he returned to the site of his original

lonely hermitage, a place very dear to him. He asked the monks not to visit, bring food or disturb him in any way. The wild animals kept him company. A wild boar which was being hunted found its way into his oratory, closely pursued by dogs and men. The huntsmen, however, on seeing the saint kneeling under a tree praying with birds perched on his shoulders and hands, were dumbfounded, and the hounds lay down and would not go after the boar. For the sake of the hermit they all went quietly away and allowed the boar to go free.

Kevin's humility was further demonstrated in that he was an abbot who chose to remain as a priest rather than become a bishop. He spent most of his life at Glendalough, unlike some of his fellow saints who travelled widely on missionary journeys, but despite this his influence and fame spread far and wide.

Nectan

FEAST DAY: 17 June

Guarding thy people, O Nectan, companion of the martyrs, Pray to the Lord for us, both now and ever. Amen.

From the Mass of St Nectan (translated from the Latin)

According to a twelfth-century Life written for Hartland Abbey, St Nectan, or Nighton as he is known in the vernacular, was the eldest and leader of the Children of Brychan and therefore Welsh by origin. The centre of his cult, however, was across the Bristol Channel at Hartland, the most north-westerly point of the Devon coast. The medieval Life goes on to tell how Nectan was inspired by the example of St Antony of Egypt, one of the Desert Fathers, who spent his life in prayer, study and manual work alone in an isolated place. Accordingly, Nectan set out on his own in a boat, committing himself and his journey to God. He sailed away, leaving behind his lands, inheritance and family, and came safely to land on the

wooded shores of Hartland, so named because of all the deer there.

After wandering a little he found a beautiful valley, green and peaceful, in which to settle. Here he made himself a shelter of tree branches and bark, and found acorns and herbs for food. Austerity and godliness were the hallmarks of his secluded life.

Gradually his brothers and sisters followed him across the water, scattering and settling in various parts of the western peninsula to lead the eremitic life. Nectan was acknowledged as their senior brother, and each year after Christmas at the Feast of the Circumcision of Our Lord they would all gather together at Stoke, where he lived, to pray and talk of the things of God.

Some distance away lived a swine-herd called Huddon. One day, while he was roaming the woods looking for his master's breeding sow and her piglets, he chanced to come upon the hermit's humble dwelling. He inquired of the saint whether he had seen the lost animals and immediately Nectan was able to show him where they were. On his return Huddon related the whole story to his master, who was moved to reward Nectan with the gift of two excellent milk-cows. Unfortunately these were stolen by two robbers. Nectan set off in search of the beasts and found them not far from his hut, at a place called Neweton. The thieves, having been discovered, beheaded Nectan. It was 17 June, which has become his feast day.

According to legend, the saint then picked up his own head and proceeded to carry it back to the well near his hut. He laid it down on a certain stone, in which red streaks said to be his blood can be seen to this day. One of the robbers went mad and died on the spot, while the other was rendered almost totally blind. He followed the headless Nectan as best he could, touching the blood of the martyr as he went, and by his action did not completely lose his sight. He buried the body with the utmost reverence inside the little hut where Nectan had lived.

The pre-Christian Celts believed that the head contained the spirit of the person, and consequently the severed head was much prized as a war trophy. Many sanctuaries and shrines had skull-niches in the

walls specifically for the display of human heads. Given that there was also a Celtic water deity called Nechtan, it seems probable that pagan elements have become muddled with Christian legend. There is a story of how one night in a certain house servants were trying to boil water over a great fire, but no matter how much wood they piled underneath it would not get hot. Finally one of them peered into the cauldron by the light of a candle and saw an eel at the bottom. He recognized it as the same one which lived in St Nectan's fountain. The eel was removed and put back in its rightful place and at once the water came to the boil.

After his death Nectan's silver bell was thrown into the waterfall in St Nectan's Glen, between Tintagel and Boscastle in Cornwall, where it buried itself beneath the water in St Nectan's Kieve, the lower of two stone basins. (A keeve is a large tub used in brewing.) This has given rise to a legend of buried treasure.

In the tenth or eleventh century Nectan's body was rediscovered. An angel appeared to a priest in a dream and told him to go with three men and enter the church of St Nectan, where they would find the body of the blessed martyr on the northern side. They were to dig it up and place it somewhere more worthy where it could be honoured. The priest in all humility did not act immediately, wanting to be sure that the message did indeed come from God. On three consecutive nights he enjoyed the same vision, so he went to report his story to Livyng, the Bishop of Crediton. Because of the priest's insignificant position, the Bishop did not give it any consideration, so the man returned home and summoned all the older devout people of the area, both priests and laymen, and recounted his visions to them. He instructed them to spend three days in fasting and prayer. At the end of this time the clergymen continued in prayer while the others took various implements with which to dig. Some while later they went to rest and the priest continued the task alone. Soon his spade struck a stone. When he moved it, a fragrant perfume issued forth and a brilliant light shone from heaven, for he had found the place where Nectan was buried.

After this discovery, Livyng repented and begged pardon for his disbelief and ingratitude. He sent as gifts two bells, a great quantity of lead for the church roof and a richly worked door. The simple pastoral staff also found in the tomb was later decorated with precious metals and jewels by the faithful parishioners, and near the body a bone seal was found with the saint's name carved on it.

The translation of Nectan's remains to a shrine took place on 4 December. Many healing miracles were attributed to the relics, which were sometimes taken on a circuit of the local countryside as far as Marhamchurch in Cornwall in one direction and almost to Barnstaple in the other. Nectan is also credited with the victory of King Aethelstan over the Scottish King Anelaus, and the deliverance of the nation from bubonic plague. In his gratitude the King gave two hides of land to the church and was ever devoted to the martyr.

There are dedications to Nectan in Devon and Cornwall as one

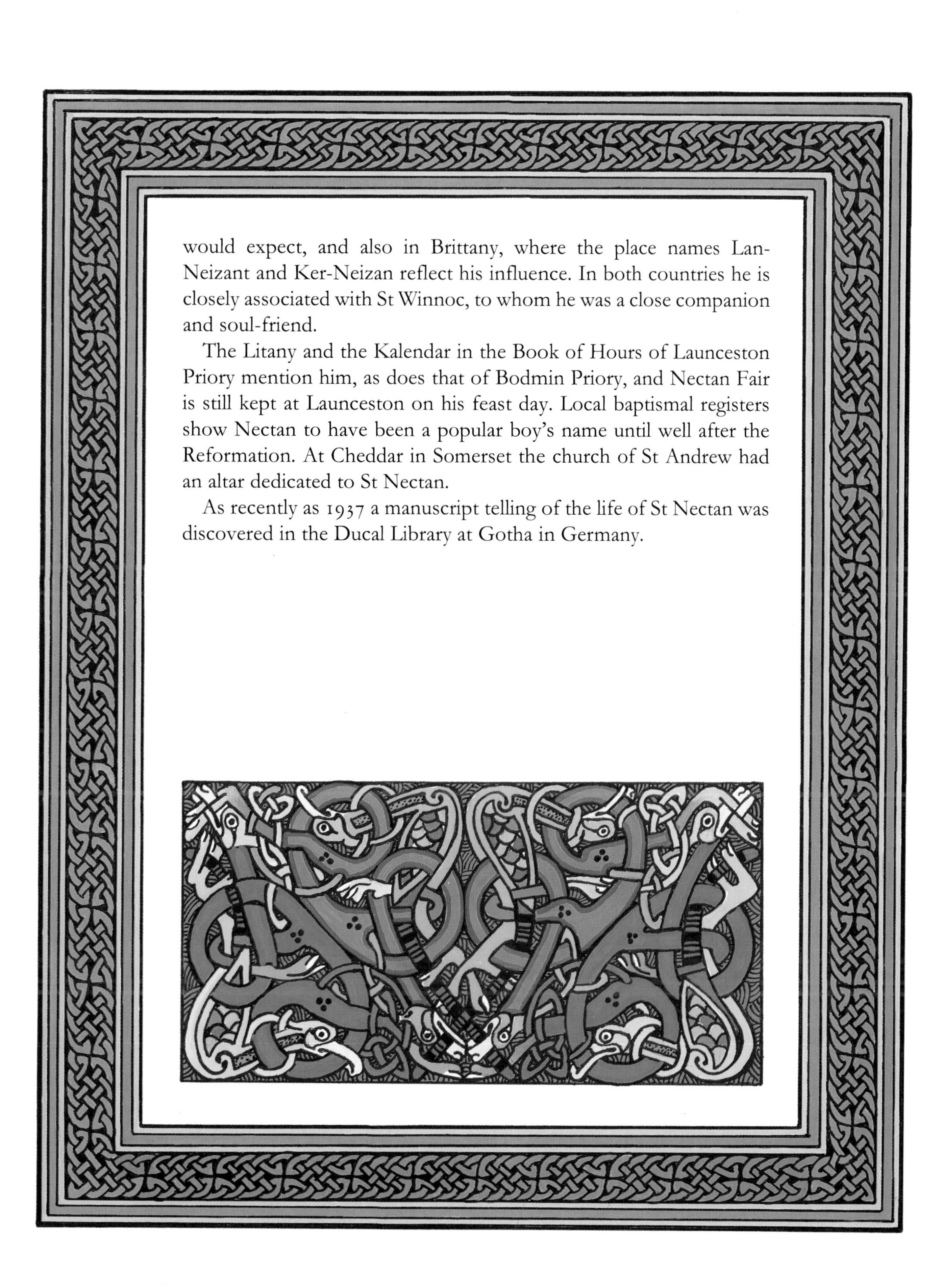

would expect, and also in Brittany, where the place names Lan-Neizant and Ker-Neizan reflect his influence. In both countries he is closely associated with St Winnoc, to whom he was a close companion and soul-friend.

The Litany and the Kalendar in the Book of Hours of Launceston Priory mention him, as does that of Bodmin Priory, and Nectan Fair is still kept at Launceston on his feast day. Local baptismal registers show Nectan to have been a popular boy's name until well after the Reformation. At Cheddar in Somerset the church of St Andrew had an altar dedicated to St Nectan.

As recently as 1937 a manuscript telling of the life of St Nectan was discovered in the Ducal Library at Gotha in Germany.

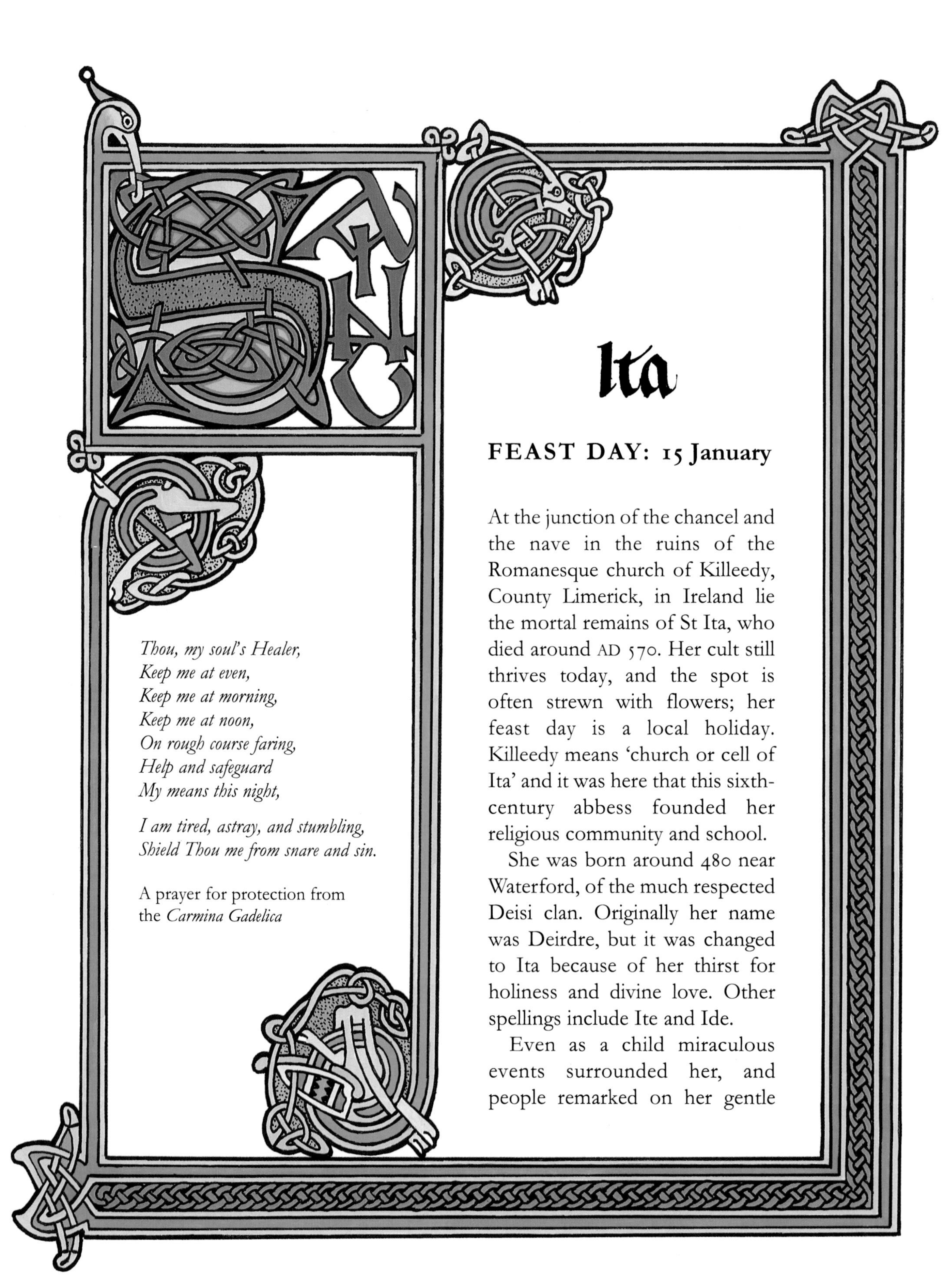

Ita

FEAST DAY: 15 January

At the junction of the chancel and the nave in the ruins of the Romanesque church of Killeedy, County Limerick, in Ireland lie the mortal remains of St Ita, who died around AD 570. Her cult still thrives today, and the spot is often strewn with flowers; her feast day is a local holiday. Killeedy means 'church or cell of Ita' and it was here that this sixth-century abbess founded her religious community and school.

She was born around 480 near Waterford, of the much respected Deisi clan. Originally her name was Deirdre, but it was changed to Ita because of her thirst for holiness and divine love. Other spellings include Ite and Ide.

Even as a child miraculous events surrounded her, and people remarked on her gentle

Thou, my soul's Healer,
Keep me at even,
Keep me at morning,
Keep me at noon,
On rough course faring,
Help and safeguard
My means this night,

I am tired, astray, and stumbling,
Shield Thou me from snare and sin.

A prayer for protection from the *Carmina Gadelica*

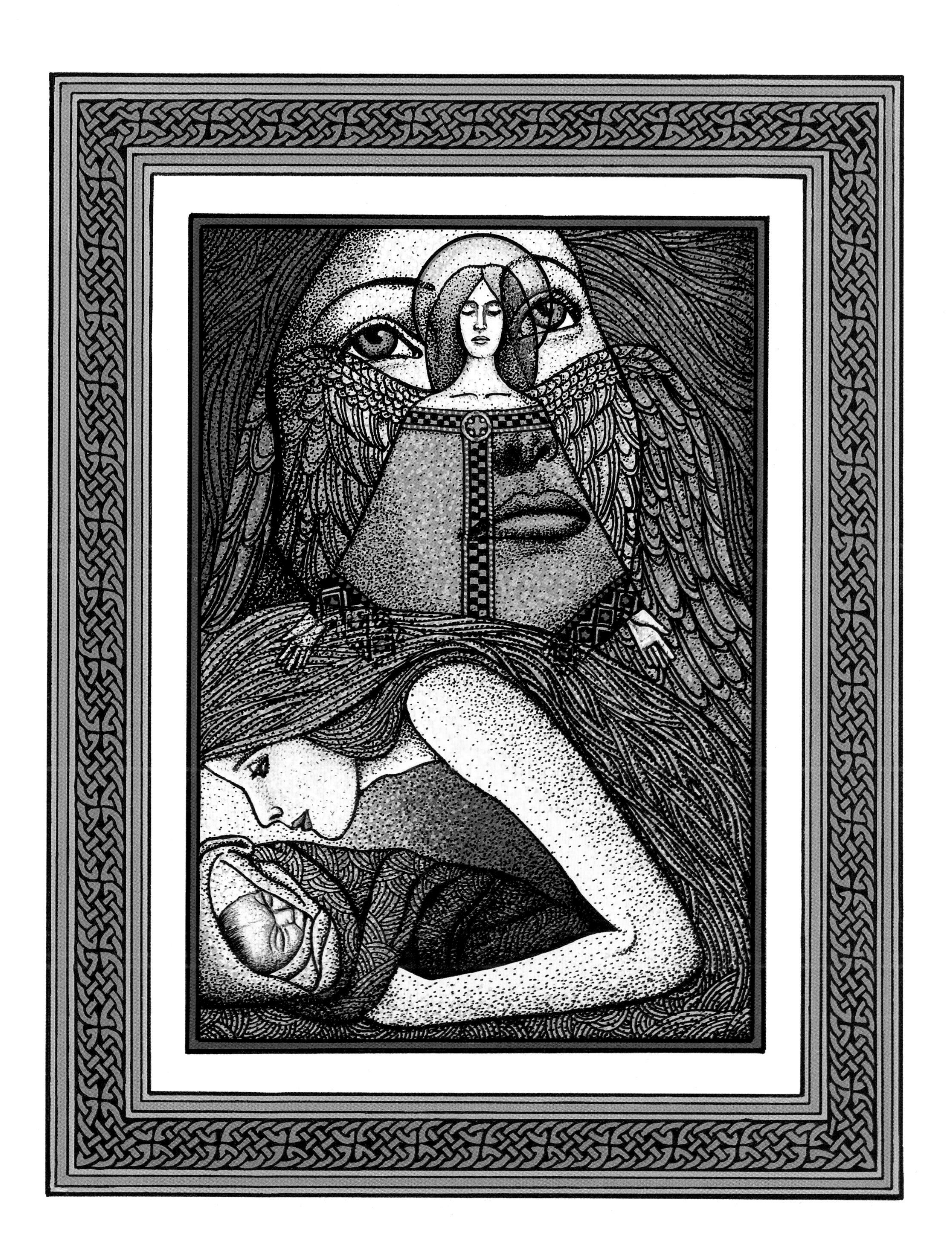

generosity, purity and gracious behaviour. One day as she was asleep in her room it seemed to other people that the whole place was on fire, but when they came to rescue her the blaze had abated. When Ita woke up, her entire form was so bright with dazzling light that they could not easily look at her. It became clear that it was the grace of God that had caused the apparent conflagration. After a while her original appearance returned.

On another occasion Ita dreamed that an angel gave her three precious stones. On waking, while she puzzled over the meaning of the message, an angel appeared to tell her that she would experience dreams and visitations throughout her earthly life and that the jewels signified the gifts of the Father, Son, and Holy Spirit to her.

Like St Bridget's, Ita's father was resistant to the new faith and when she reached a certain age a marriage was arranged for her with a suitable young man, also of noble birth. Due to her fasting and prayers, however, an angel appeared prophesying that she would serve God in another part of the country and that many would find salvation because of her. Her family were duly persuaded to allow her to move away and settle near the foot of Sliabh Luachra, where she was joined by other women who also wished to live the religious life. The people of Ui Conaill came with their chieftain, offering her much land, but she took only four acres for a vegetable garden. The local people continued to bring alms and gifts regularly to support the community.

The main vocation in the life of this 'second Bridget', as one writer describes her, was to make known the saints as 'soul-friends' to her nuns and pupils. The concept of the 'soul-friend' was an important one in Celtic Christianity. It came to the Celtic church through Egypt and North Africa and was someone who was an intimate confidante, confessor and spiritual director. Sometimes the soul-friend was one who had already died and was in the spirit, thus linking this world and the next.

Ita's chosen lifestyle was very rigorous, and an angel was sent to warn her about her excessive fasting; she sometimes went without

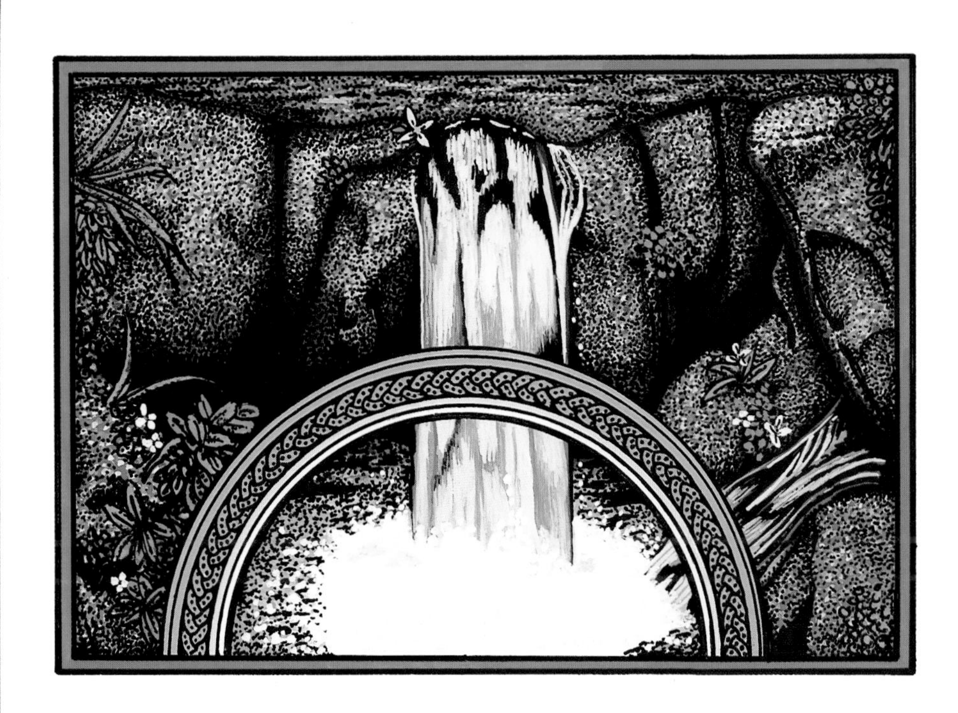

food for up to four days at a time, which made her very weak with hunger. She did not wish to forgo this practice, however, so she was supplied, by the mercy of God, with heavenly food which she could not refuse from that day until her death. As well as fasting, she spent long periods in solitary prayer and meditation during her ascetic life. She also possessed gifts of prophecy and healing and was much sought after as an adviser and counsellor. The waters of her nearby holy well were reputed through the centuries to cure smallpox and other diseases.

As part of the purpose of her foundation, Ita set up an educational establishment for young boys; by tradition, St Brendan was one of her pupils. In the eighth-century poem by Alcuin of York she is called 'the foster-mother of all the saints of Ireland'. Brendan is said to have asked her what were the three things that most pleased and displeased God. She replied with characteristic wisdom, saying that a pure heart with faith in God, a simple life with religious spirit, and generous charity inspired by love most delighted him, and a mouth that hates people, a heart harbouring resentments, and a confidence in material wealth most offended him.

One of the strangest but also most popular stories told about Ita is that she prayed that God's son from heaven might be given to her in the form of a human baby to nurse. Subsequently she was granted this in a vision, and thus shares with St Bridget the title of being 'the wet-nurse of Christ'. The composition of an Irish lullaby for the infant Jesus has been attributed to her.

Like many Celtic saints, Ita knew when she was going to die. There were messengers on the way to her from Clonmacnoise to ask her to bless water for their abbot, Aengus, who was very ill. She duly blessed some water, telling her sisters that she would die before the messengers arrived and that Aengus would also die before they could return to him. And so it happened.

A true soul-friend and confessor to many, there are dedications to Ita in Cornwall as well as in Ireland, and she was even invoked in ancient litanies on the Continent.

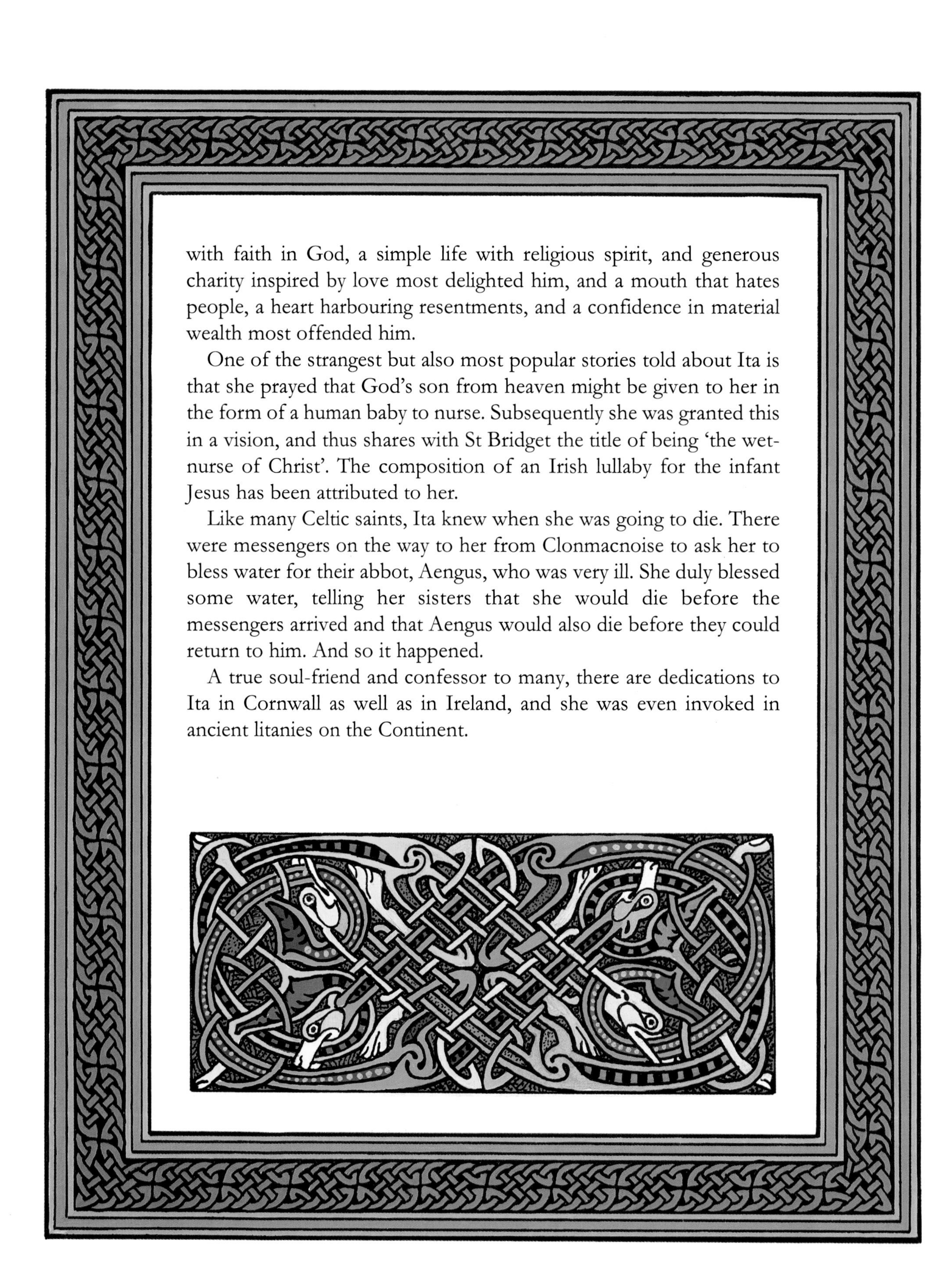

Winwaloe

FEAST DAY: 3 March

This saint is a fine illustration of the close links that existed between the Celtic peoples, in this case Brittany and Cornwall, during the Age of the Saints. There are various forms of his name, the most common being Winwaloe, Gunwalloe, or Guénolé, meaning 'he who is fair', not necessarily in features but with an inner beauty which shines through.

He came of a Cornish family which had fled to Brittany and settled there to avoid the Saxon encroachment, and he was born near St Brieuc. His mother, Gwen, and his father, Fracan, (whose name survives in the parish of Winwaloe's birth, Ploufragan), vowed that their third son should be dedicated to God. However, it was not until

Almighty God, by whose grace the blessed Abbot Winwaloe became a burning and shining light in your church; kindle in us the same spirit of discipline and love that we may ever walk before you as children of light, through Jesus Christ our Lord. Amen.

Collect for St Winwaloe

the boy was fifteen years of age that he and his two brothers, Gwethenoc and Jacut, went to join the monastery of St Budoc on the island of Lavret, part of the Île de Bréhat.

After some years his brothers returned to their old life, but Winwaloe, being both a willing and an able pupil, continued as a monk. His friend and teacher, Budoc, appreciated in him the marks of holiness and saintliness in his Christian life, so when the time came to found a new community he was sent out with eleven other brothers to establish it. This was the custom in the Celtic church, so that communities were rarely large and the gospel was spread abroad.

Initially they settled on the island of Tibidy, where they eked out a living feeding on roots and herbs and a little barley that they found growing there. For three years the band of monks endured this hardship, but eventually the infertility of the soil and the violence of the winds forced them to seek an alternative site. It is said that Winwaloe had a vision of angels ascending and descending on the opposite shore of the River Aulne; it appeared to be so much like Paradise that they moved across there and so the great monastery of Landévennec was founded. Another story says that life on Tibidy was so good and pleasant that the monks would not, or could not, die, so to give them release from this earthly life they left the island. Gradlon, whose tomb can still be seen at Landévennec, granted them land to found their monstery on his estate of Tévenec.

As in all Celtic monastic communities, the life was an austere one. Wine and wheat were not used except as the elements of the Mass. Instead they drank only water, sometimes mixed with wild herbs, and ate only barley bread with boiled roots, except on Sundays and feast

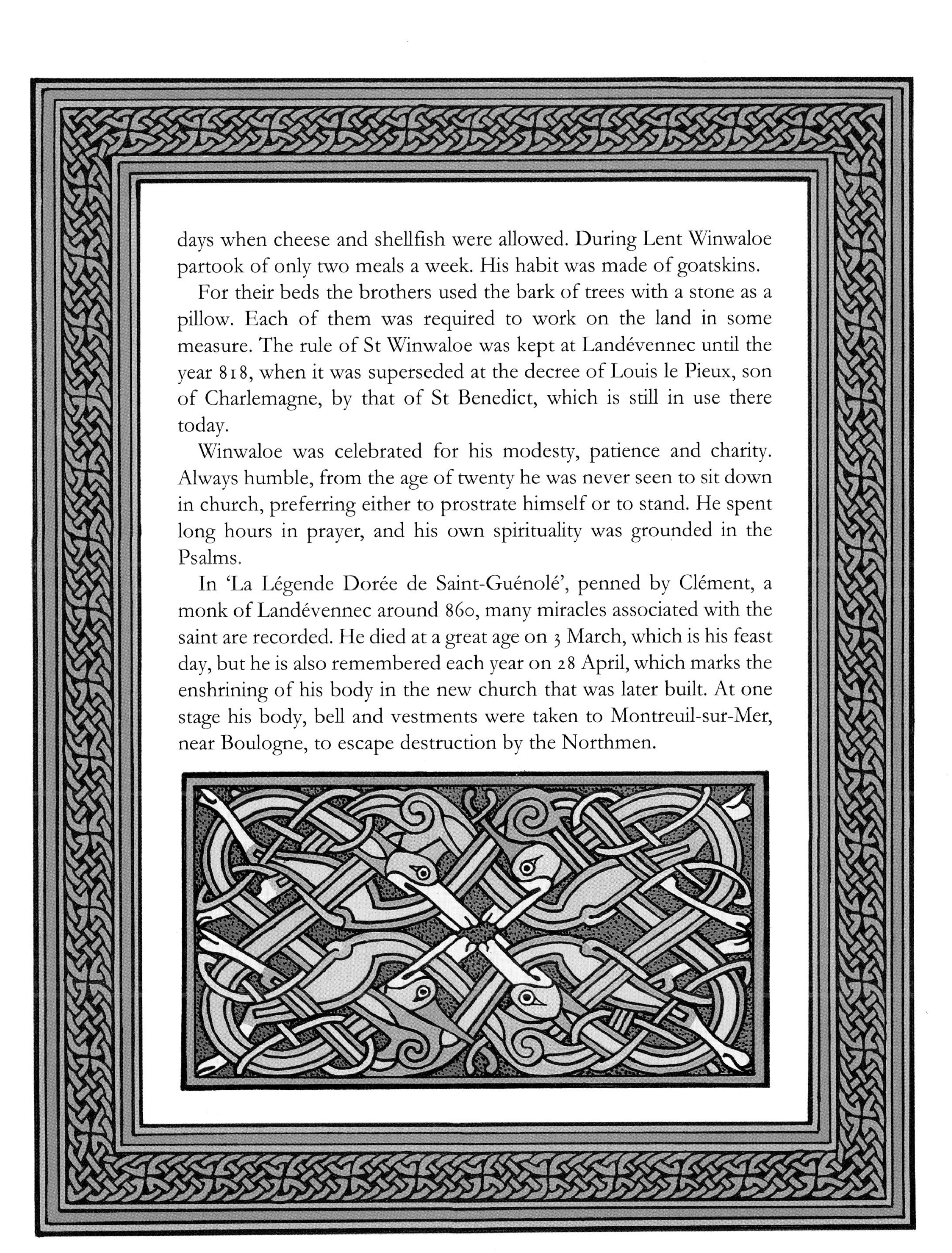

days when cheese and shellfish were allowed. During Lent Winwaloe partook of only two meals a week. His habit was made of goatskins.

For their beds the brothers used the bark of trees with a stone as a pillow. Each of them was required to work on the land in some measure. The rule of St Winwaloe was kept at Landévennec until the year 818, when it was superseded at the decree of Louis le Pieux, son of Charlemagne, by that of St Benedict, which is still in use there today.

Winwaloe was celebrated for his modesty, patience and charity. Always humble, from the age of twenty he was never seen to sit down in church, preferring either to prostrate himself or to stand. He spent long hours in prayer, and his own spirituality was grounded in the Psalms.

In 'La Légende Dorée de Saint-Guénolé', penned by Clément, a monk of Landévennec around 860, many miracles associated with the saint are recorded. He died at a great age on 3 March, which is his feast day, but he is also remembered each year on 28 April, which marks the enshrining of his body in the new church that was later built. At one stage his body, bell and vestments were taken to Montreuil-sur-Mer, near Boulogne, to escape destruction by the Northmen.

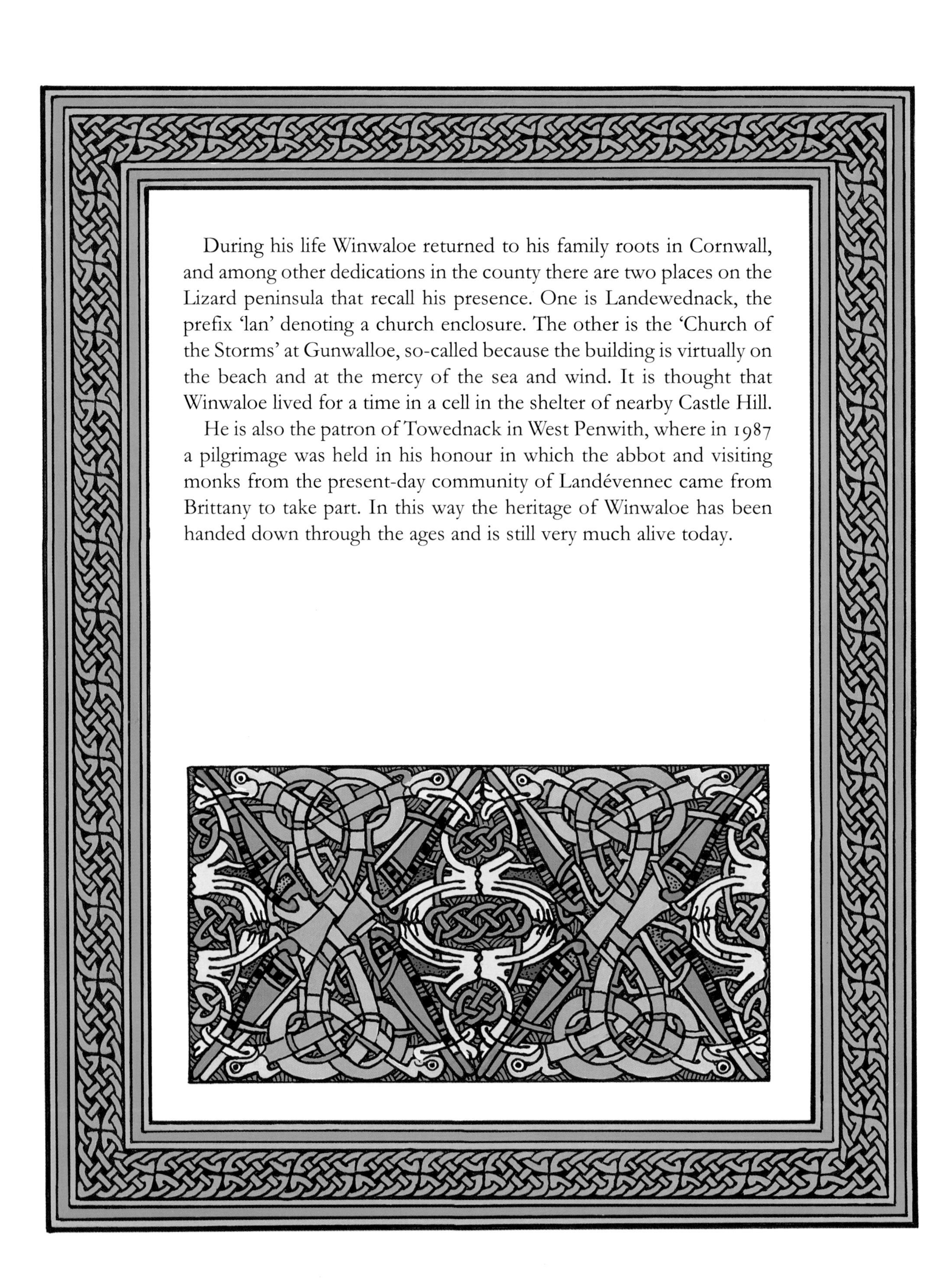

During his life Winwaloe returned to his family roots in Cornwall, and among other dedications in the county there are two places on the Lizard peninsula that recall his presence. One is Landewednack, the prefix 'lan' denoting a church enclosure. The other is the 'Church of the Storms' at Gunwalloe, so-called because the building is virtually on the beach and at the mercy of the sea and wind. It is thought that Winwaloe lived for a time in a cell in the shelter of nearby Castle Hill.

He is also the patron of Towednack in West Penwith, where in 1987 a pilgrimage was held in his honour in which the abbot and visiting monks from the present-day community of Landévennec came from Brittany to take part. In this way the heritage of Winwaloe has been handed down through the ages and is still very much alive today.

SOURCES AND INSPIRATION FOR THE ILLUSTRATIONS

Page 3 Based on the Soiscel Molaise book shrine, from Devenish Island, County Fermanagh, AD 1000.
Page 4 The chapel of St Catherine, Abbotsbury, Dorset.
Page 5 St Pedry's Well, Treloy, Cornwall.
Page 8 Eighth-century bell shrine fragment.
Page 10 Detail from the Book of Lindisfarne, AD 698.
Page 13 Self-portrait.
Page 17 The largest of the sixth-century dry-stone monastic cells on Skellig, County Kerry.
Page 17 Border from the Lindisfarne Gospels.
Page 18 Detail from the eleventh-century shrine of the Breac Maodhog. The early monastery of Sceilg Mhichil, viewed from the beehive cells on top of the Great Skellig Rock.
Page 19 Eighth-century Crucifixion plaque from St John's, Rinnigan, County Roscommon.
Page 23 The eighth-century Monymusk shrine, which once contained a relic of St Columba.
Page 26 The path St Columba must have trodden to the site of the Scotic kings of Dalriada at Dunadd, Argyll.
Page 29 St Bridget.
Page 31 A stone decorated with a cross lying on the old midsummer pilgrimage station at Aighan, County Donegal.
Page 32 Bird panel from the Book of Kells.
Page 37 St Patrick.
Page 39 Panel design.
Page 41 Panels from the Lindisfarne Gospels.
Page 42 Panels from the Book of Kells.
Page 43 Design based on a detail from the Lindisfarne Gospels.
Page 44 Adapted from a carpet page in the Book of Durrow, AD 680.
Page 47 St Aidan.
Page 49 Entwined dogs from the Book of Kells.
Page 52 Based on various details from the Books of Kells and Lindisfarne.
Page 55 St David.
Page 56 Twelfth-century Doorty Cross at Kilfenora, County Clare.
Page 58 Key pattern panel.
Page 61 St Michael, eighth/ninth-century Irish mount of an angel with a sword possibly depicting St Michael. St Michael's tower on the summit of Glastonbury Tor, the only remains of a church which was destroyed by earthquake.
Page 62 The chapel at Roche Rock, Cornwall, which is dedicated to St Michael.
Page 64 Panel based upon various details from the Lindisfarne Gospels.
Page 67 St Cuthbert.
Page 70 Knotwork cross panel.
Page 72 First-century gold torque.
Page 73 St Winefride.
Page 77 St Kentigern.
Page 79 Based on a page from the seventh-century Book of Durrow.
Page 80 Tenth-century St Martin's Cross, one of the few survivors of the 360 crosses which stood on St Columba's island.
Page 82 Bird panel.
Page 85 St Petroc.
Page 86 Detail of a bishop on the twelfth-century cross at Dysert O'Dea, County Clare.
Page 88 Spiral panel based on detail from the Book of Kells.
Page 91 St Piran's Well at Trethevy, near Tintagel, which stands beside the pilgrim's way leading to St Nectan's Glen.
Page 92 Detail from St Buryan's cross and the wayside Three Holes cross from Cornwall.
Page 94 Step pattern panel based on a detail from the Lindisfarne Gospels.
Page 97 St Ia.
Page 98 Entwined dogs panel.
Page 101 St Kevin: the twelfth-century remains of the presumed tomb shrine of St Kevin at Glendalough.
Page 103 The entrance to St Nun's Well at Pelynt, Cornwall.
Page 105 Cross panel based on details from the Books of Kells and Lindisfarne.
Page 107 St Nectan.
Page 109 A bronze figure mounted on St Manchan's shrine, AD 1130.
Page 113 St Ita.
Page 115 St Edith's Well, Stoke Edith, near Hereford.
Page 117 Based on a detail from one of the carpet pages in the Lindisfarne Gospels.
Page 119 St Winwaloe.
Page 121 Entwined dogs.
Page 123 Cross panel.
Page 128 Design based on a spiral panel on the Hilton of Cadboll Stone, Ross-shire.

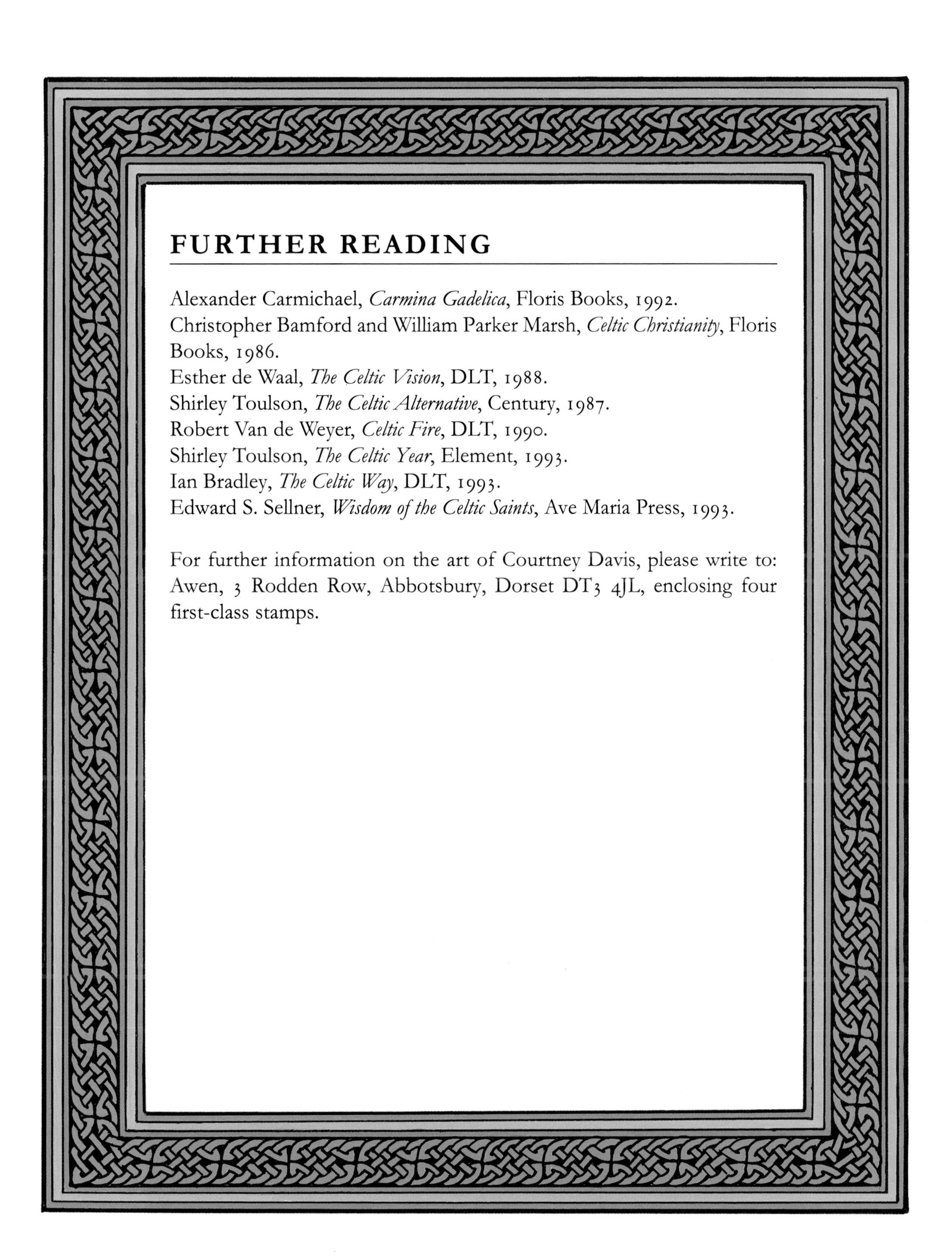

FURTHER READING

Alexander Carmichael, *Carmina Gadelica*, Floris Books, 1992.
Christopher Bamford and William Parker Marsh, *Celtic Christianity*, Floris Books, 1986.
Esther de Waal, *The Celtic Vision*, DLT, 1988.
Shirley Toulson, *The Celtic Alternative*, Century, 1987.
Robert Van de Weyer, *Celtic Fire*, DLT, 1990.
Shirley Toulson, *The Celtic Year*, Element, 1993.
Ian Bradley, *The Celtic Way*, DLT, 1993.
Edward S. Sellner, *Wisdom of the Celtic Saints*, Ave Maria Press, 1993.

For further information on the art of Courtney Davis, please write to: Awen, 3 Rodden Row, Abbotsbury, Dorset DT3 4JL, enclosing four first-class stamps.

INDEX